# THE INSIDER'S GUIDE TO

# MANAGING

## YOUR

# CREDIT

## HOW TO ESTABLISH, MAINTAIN, REPAIR, AND PROTECT YOUR CREDIT

### DEBORAH MCNAUGHTON

D1568429

Dearborn
Financial Publishing, Inc.®

This publication is designed to provide accurate and authoritative information in regard to the subject matter covered. It is sold with the understanding that the publisher is not engaged in rendering legal, accounting, or other professional service. If legal advice or other expert assistance is required, the services of a competent professional person should be sought.

Editorial Director: Cynthia A. Zigmund
Managing Editor: Jack Kiburz
Interior Design: Lucy Jenkins
Cover Design: DePinto Studios
Typesetting: Elizabeth Pitts

**Library of Congress Cataloging-in-Publication Data**

McNaughton, Deborah, 1950–
    The insider's guide to managing your credit : how to establish, maintain, repair, and protect your credit / Deborah McNaughton.
        p.  cm.
    Includes index.
    ISBN 0-7931-2669-X (pbk)
    1. Consumer credit—United States.   I. Title.
HG3756.U54M363   1997
332.7'48–dc21                                                97-28260
                                                            CIP

Dearborn books are available at special quantity discounts to use as premiums and sales promotions, or for use in corporate training programs. For more information, please call the Special Sales Manager at 800-621-9621, ext. 4384, or write to Dearborn Financial Publishing, Inc., 155 North Wacker Drive, Chicago, IL 60606-1719.

## Praise for *The Insider's Guide to Managing Your Credit*

"Every time you pay us a visit, the phone lines are jammed with calls. And—our listeners are so grateful for the help you give them. We get top newsmakers on our show, but you join an elite circle of the top response-getters. The welcome mat is always out!"

> —Warren Duffy, Radio talk show host
> Duffy and Company "Live from L.A."

"Deborah McNaughton once again demonstrates that she is America's most talented and prolific financial service writer. Her clear, concise, easily understood prose reveals a background steeped in research and practical experience. I recommend her book for anyone about to embark in the treacherous waters of loans and family finance. May God keep her treading these waters for many years to come."

> —Merwin C. Ellis, President
> Credi-Care, Inc.
> America's Largest Debt Consolidation Service

"*The Insider's Guide to Managing Your Credit* is the only book you'll ever need about credit. Whether you are just starting out, facing some credit problems, or rebuilding after a financial disaster, this book gives you all the tools you need to guide you through the complicated world of credit. I especially like the worksheets and sample letters because they offer simple, straightforward, effective, and easy-to-understand solutions that will help you take charge of and manage any credit situation."

> —Paul Navestad, President and Chief Executive Officer
> Financial Services Network–USA, Inc.

"Wow! *The Insider's Guide to Managing Your Credit* is an absolutely indispensable tool to assist anyone to get through the credit maze that is life in the 1990s. Whatever your age group, from those just starting out, to those who are already lost and trying to cope, this book will inform, help clarify, and empower you with a plan of action! I strongly recommend this book. Indeed, if you hope to have a chance to be successful and enjoy peace of mind, it should be considered required reading!"

–Larry Py, General Manager
Coast Cadillac
The Fastest Growing Cadillac Dealership in Southern California


"Deborah McNaughton's book *The Insider's Guide to Managing Your Credit* is must reading for those who need help in correcting inaccurate credit reports, which can affect consumer credit, employment, and insurance opportunities. Ms. McNaughton, who is the country's leading expert on credit reports, turns on the light that has been darkened by government regulation. Now consumers have the help they need to protect their rights under federal laws regulating credit bureaus."

–Jerome S. Lamet
Attorney at Law


"Deborah McNaughton arms her readers with all the tools they need to establish and maintain the best credit record possible. Her step-by-step instructions are invaluable for those having difficulty with the credit system, helping them deal with credit reporting agencies and bill collectors in the best possible way."

–Jordan E. Goodman
Author, *Everyone's Money Book*


"An informative, essential tool for all who, at one time or another, are faced with the credit maze. Ms. McNaughton has succeeded with an easy-to-understand reference that is second to none. I recommend it as must reading for all who depend upon credit personally or in business."

–Robert A. Bonito
Attorney at Law

"A *must* for all young adults as well as other credit users to read to keep themselves out of trouble. If you keep this book handy, you can save yourself a lot of problems."

> —James Frannea, President
> Consumer Credit Counseling Service of Orange County

"You will find this book helpful and informative. I use it as a resource at my current station and have recommended it to many others."

> —P. Steven Roa, Area Sales Development Manager, Northern California
> Great Western Bank

## Dedication

To Hal, who always encourages my writing; my three daughters, Tiffany, Christy, and Mindy; my two sons-in-law, Mike and Kyle; and my grandson Austin

And to the thousands of individuals whom I have counseled, who have learned from the past and await a new future in the world of credit

# Contents

## PART THREE
## Credit Restoration/Credit Repair

# Preface

John was frantic when he called my credit consulting office. He was 21 years old and had never had credit. He had made several applications to credit card companies but was turned down because he had no payment history. How could he get credit when he had never established credit?

Mary called the office one afternoon in a state of panic because she was behind on her bills. Bill collectors were constantly contacting her. Collection agencies were harassing her. She couldn't sleep and was a nervous wreck. What could she do?

Martin, concerned and upset, called the office because he had been denied credit as a result of negative, but inaccurate, entries on his credit report. Even though the credit report was not accurate, Martin couldn't establish new credit. What could he do to correct the inaccuracies?

The questions above are typical of ones received by credit consulting offices throughout the United States.

Credit is a way of life. In today's society, without credit you cannot qualify for a house, a car, credit cards, bank loans, and many other things. The list is endless. You can't rent a car or secure a hotel reservation without a credit card. Why then is it that so many people get into trouble once they obtain credit?

People do not realize the importance of establishing credit and the responsibility of maintaining a good credit report. Many people feel by using credit they can always pay tomorrow. That, however, is the wrong attitude. Paying tomorrow will only cause excessive debt. There is a right way and a wrong way to use credit. One of the main objectives of this book is to teach you the correct way to establish credit and to use it to your advantage.

With economic conditions shifting back and forth, many individuals are encountering problems with their finances. Credit card companies, banks, and savings and loan companies are suffering financial losses because consumers are not able to pay their bills.

The following pages provide information on all areas of credit that is recession proof. The book is divided into three parts. Part One covers all areas of establishing credit. Part Two deals with credit problems and their solutions, and getting out of debt. Part Three tells you how to dispute inaccurate information listed on your credit report. Knowing what your legal rights are and how to get assistance is important in establishing credit and solving credit problems.

The worksheets included in this book will help you know where you are in the credit world. By completing each sheet you will be able to identify what your needs may be. If you recognize areas in your credit life that need improvement, you'll be able to identify them by completing the questionnaires.

High schools and colleges rarely teach the importance of credit. When you enter the adult world without knowledge, credit disaster will inevitably strike. Frequently, clients who have come for credit consulting, will say, "If I had only known the importance of maintaining a good credit record, I would have done things differently."

Many unscrupulous businesses have appeared in the marketplace claiming to be credit experts. Thousands of individuals have fallen prey to these companies only to find they were not legitimate. Companies have disappeared with clients' money without doing what they promised to do. Needing assistance with credit problems is devastating to an individual. It is like an emotional roller coaster. Desperation leads an individual to anybody that has solutions. BEWARE! Some legitimate companies are out there, but armed with the information in this book, you will get the answers you need without spending hundreds, or even thousands, of dollars.

Establishing credit, dealing with credit problems, and restoring your credit report are topics everyone can benefit from knowing about.

Be patient and persistent in reaching your goals in the credit world. Nothing happens overnight, but with careful planning and research, you will reach your goal.

Nothing in this book is intended as legal assistance or legal advice. Materials have been carefully researched to increase your credit knowledge. Names of individuals are fictitious to protect their identity.

# Part One

# Establishing Credit

# Chapter 1

# Plan Your Future!
## Setting Your Credit Priorities

## Credit versus Debt

A biblical proverb warns, "Do not be a man who strikes hands in pledge or puts up security for debts: if you lack the means to pay, your very bed will be snatched from under you" (Prov. 22:26,27 NIV). A person who owes several debts at the same time always runs the risk of overextending. A balance between obtaining credit and being debt free must be found.

*Credit* is defined as trustworthiness, or credibility. It encompasses the time allowed for payment for goods or services obtained on trust. Confidence in a purchaser's ability and intention to pay is shown by entrusting that purchaser with goods or services without immediate payment.

*Debt* is defined as something that is owed to someone. It is something that one person is bound to pay to, or perform for, another—a liability or obligation to pay or render something.

Obtaining credit is an art. Most people do not realize the importance of filling out an application for credit correctly. There would be fewer denials of credit if the average consumer, before filling out the application, knew what the potential credit grantor looks for.

It is important not to become an impulsive buyer with credit. An impulsive buyer is one who has to purchase an item right at that moment without thought of how the balance will be paid. The buyer never thinks that his or her source of money may be cut off—a sure way to fall into debt. Falling too far into debt may cause family problems, divorce, and anxiety over paying back creditors.

The key to this book is to be trustworthy with the credit you receive. Set goals of being debt free. Be responsible with the credit you obtain. Learn to make money with your credit. Invest your money wisely. Do not become impulsive with your credit cards. Always pay your balances when they're due. The only time to draw out your payments is when you are establishing credit and building a positive payment pattern.

You do not have to be in debt to have credit. By paying your accounts off monthly, you will avoid going into debt.

## Goals for Credit Needs

It is important to know in what direction you're headed when dealing with credit matters. Setting goals for your credit needs is just as important as setting goals for your life. It requires a plan of action to accomplish each step. As you accomplish each goal, you will gain confidence in setting new ones.

You need to determine what advantages you gain from credit. Listed are some possibilities:

- A mortgage or equity loan for a home
- A line of credit for a business
- Credit for personal use such as buying a car, boat, or motor vehicle
- A student loan
- Material gain
- Cash

An examination of each possibility follows.

### Home

A home is probably the largest investment an individual will make in his or her entire life. To qualify for a home mortgage or equity line of credit, an individual must be creditworthy. Without a good credit history indicating a good payment pattern, you cannot qualify. If there have been problems with your past payment pattern, you may not qualify for the best interest rate and terms or not qualify at all. Having credit is a must in qualifying for a mortgage. You don't have to be in debt with outstanding balances owed. The credit report needs to show only that you have made your payments on time. The less money you owe, the better your qualification.

## Business

Establishing a line of credit for a business is often needed for starting a business or to have a line of credit on reserve for future improvements or possible problems. Establishing credit for a business can be done through your bank or through a credit card with a large credit line.

When applying for a line of credit with a bank, remember a bank will not look at your application unless you have established a good payment history that is shown on your credit report. If you are unable to qualify for a bank loan or decide not to apply for a loan, you, like many business people, may use your credit card for cash advances. The interest rates, however, are usually higher than for bank loans. By using the line of credit from your credit card, you can request an increase of your credit limit, providing the account is current and in good standing.

## Personal Use

Establishing credit for personal use, such as owning an automobile, boat, or any type of motor vehicle, still requires past credit experience. Occasionally, some finance companies will let you establish credit even if you have never had it or have had negative credit. The cost of the loan and interest rates under those circumstances are substantially higher. An automobile purchase is probably the second largest investment you will make. If you can't pay cash for the automobile, try to pay the loan off as quickly as possible.

The purchase of a boat or another motor vehicle is handled the same as an automobile, although the length of repayment may be shorter or longer. The finance company will evaluate what it will do according to your past credit history. If you have had past credit problems, you may get a higher interest rate and be required to pay a large down payment.

## Student Loans

With the rising cost of college, more and more students need student loans to complete their education. Many banks have special programs that offer students financial assistance. Many of these programs are government loans under which students defer making payments until several months after they graduate or leave school. The interest rates are usually low on this type of loan, but qualification is required. Establishing past credit is a criterion. If you have a child entering college, you may have to qualify for the loan.

## Material Gain

Establishing credit for material gain refers to department store charge cards, travel and entertainment cards, and major credit cards. Using lines of credit from such cards, many people purchase items with an attitude of "buy now, pay later." Those types of cards are frequently used for purchases of major appliances.

Credit cards for material gain can either make or break you—"break" you because they'll tempt you to overextend your capacity to repay debts, but "make" you because they're the cards credit grantors will verify through your credit report to check your paying habits and ability to establish new credit. If your habits are good and you are not overextended, you have a greater possibility of being approved for new credit. If the accounts reflect a poor payment pattern and you are overextended, chances are you will not be approved for new credit. Always pay off your accounts as soon as possible to avoid the possibility of a credit rejection. You never know when an emergency may arise and you need to establish new credit or increase the lines of credit you already have.

## Cash

Cash from a line of credit is always useful in paying off your debts (providing your payments will be reduced), starting a business, purchasing personal items, taking a family vacation, and so on. The key is qualification and making sure you can pay the loan off as agreed.

## Setting Goals

*Goals* can be defined as the end result of an achievement toward which effort is directed. You need to evaluate what it is you want and do everything possible to make your goal a reality. Doing your homework and setting a plan of action can make the goal much easier to accomplish.

Setting goals is not an easy thing to do. It is time-consuming. *Procrastination* is a habit that will slow you down in reaching your goals. You need to follow through and set your sights on goals that are reachable. Credit is no different. Careful planning and being responsible will give you the boost you need to build a successful credit portfolio.

Several steps must be taken to make goal setting for credit needs a success. You must define those areas in which you want credit assistance. Look at the list in the previous section to see if these are areas of credit you wish to establish. You may have other credit needs—for example, credit problems or correcting a credit report, two areas covered in later sections.

Be specific in your goals. After determining what areas of credit you desire, complete the *Master Credit Goal Worksheet.* List the types of credit you may need; if it is a home loan, for example, list the mortgage amount. If you need a credit card, such as a Visa® or MasterCard® card, list the number of cards you wish to have and the credit limits you want. If the credit is for an automobile or other vehicle, list the amount you want to have financed. If the credit is for a student loan, list the amount. For department store charge cards, list the credit limit you want. Don't make unrealistic goals that leave you overextended. Make sure your income can support the credit payments. It's better to have only a few open lines of credit with a zero balance for qualification. Save your lines of credit for an emergency.

### Ten Steps to Goal Setting

**Step 1: Write your goal down on a piece of paper.** Don't try to carry your goal as a thought only—put it in writing. That will subconsciously commit you to following through on the goal. By writing it down, you are making a commitment to do something.

**Step 2. Visualize your goal.** You should cut out a picture of what you want; it may be a house, a car, or an appliance. Whatever it is, cut a picture of it from a magazine and put the picture in a place where you can see it for reinforcement.

**Step 3. Set a time frame within which you want to accomplish the goal.** Remember when establishing credit that it can take several months to get approval. Be realistic in setting dates.

**Step 4. Write out your plan of action.** When establishing credit, you need to know what institutions you are applying to. List their names, addresses, and phone numbers. Write what type of credit you are trying to obtain. Complete the *Credit Plan of Action Worksheet.*

**Step 5. Don't make excuses for not following through on your goal.** Get rid of these phrases: "I'm too busy"; "I don't have time"; "I'll do it later." If you do today what you *can* put off for tomorrow, you'll feel much better.

**Step 6. Anticipate situations that may cause you to stop moving ahead.** If you know of anything in your credit portfolio that could cause a problem, find a way to correct it, perhaps through an updated credit report.

**Step 7. Define your motives.** Are your intentions to build a credit portfolio for the future or for material gain only? You must determine the answer before you send out your first application. If the motive is for material gain only, *do not send it!*

**Step 8. Look at all your past experiences.** Learn from them. Do not be afraid of failure. You can't fail if you have learned what not to do.

**Step 9. Believe you can accomplish what you start out to do.** If things don't come out the way you want the first time, find the reason why and correct the problem.

**Step 10. Do first things first.** Don't dwell on what you need to do. Just do it! Follow through with your plan of action.

In goal setting, you must establish both long-range goals and short-range goals. Short-range goals must be accomplished before you can move to long-range goals.

Setting short-range goals with credit would include establishing a good payment pattern for your credit report. Most credit grantors like to see a good payment pattern for the past two years. The creditor's decision is based on the type of credit you are applying for.

Succeeding with a long-range goal is the result of achieving short-range goals in establishing a good credit history. A long-range goal in establishing credit would be a large purchase, such as a house, a business, or specific investments. By becoming creditworthy, you will have greater opportunity to make more money.

A short-range goal will give you more confidence to try reaching your long-range goals. Establishing goals will save you time and produce enthusiasm to start your day. Everybody looks forward to new challenges. Building a good credit portfolio is something that you will live with for the rest of your life.

A biblical proverb says, "Plans fail for lack of counsel, but with many advisers they succeed" (Prov. 15:22 NIV). You must have knowledge in credit matters. It is a necessity of life. If you are prepared when applying for credit, your chances of approval will be much higher.

Completing the following questionnaire and worksheets will help you set your own credit goals.

## Goal Setting Questionnaire

To be successful in setting goals, you must define the direction you are going. Answer the following questions before you set your goals.

1. What goals can you visualize accomplishing?

_____

_____

_____

2. Have you cut out pictures of your goals? List them.

_____

_____

_____

_____

3. Can you set a reasonable time frame in which to accomplish your goals?

_____

_____

_____

4. What excuses can you eliminate that will keep you from setting your goals?

_____

_____

_____

5. What problems can arise that will cause you to be turned down for credit?

_____

_____

_____

_____

**Goal Setting Questionnaire (Continued)**

6. Define your motives in establishing credit. Are they for the future or for material gain?

_____

_____

_____

_____

7. Is there anything in your past credit experience that can lead to credit denial? If so, list the problems.

_____

_____

_____

_____

8. If you had problems in the past, how can they be solved?

_____

_____

_____

_____

9. Do you believe you can build up your credit portfolio?

_____

_____

_____

_____

10. Are there any problems in getting started with accomplishing your goals? If so, list them.

_____

_____

_____

_____

## Master Credit Goal Worksheet

From the list below choose the type of credit you wish to have.

Mortgage or equity loan for a home

Line of credit for a business

Credit for personal use such as buying a car, boat, or motor vehicle

Student loan

Material gain

Cash

Other

| Goal or Need | Credit Amount | Number of Credit Cards Desired |
|---|---|---|
| | | |
| | | |
| | | |
| | | |
| | | |
| | | |
| | | |
| | | |
| | | |
| | | |
| | | |
| | | |
| | | |
| | | |
| | | |
| | | |
| | | |
| | | |

## Credit Plan of Action Worksheet

List the institutions and types of credit desired.

| Creditor's Name/Address | Telephone Number | Type of Credit |
|---|---|---|
| | | |
| | | |
| | | |
| | | |
| | | |
| | | |
| | | |
| | | |
| | | |
| | | |
| | | |
| | | |
| | | |
| | | |
| | | |
| | | |
| | | |
| | | |
| | | |
| | | |
| | | |
| | | |
| | | |
| | | |
| | | |
| | | |
| | | |

## One-Month Goals Worksheet

Goal                                                                    Date

## One-Year Goals Worksheet

**Goal**                                                    **Date**

## Two-Year Goals Worksheet

**Goal**                                                                          **Date**

# Five-Year Goals Worksheet

**Goal**                                                                                   **Date**

# Progress of Goals Worksheet

**Goal** . . . . . . . . . . **Date Started**                                    **Date Achieved**

# Chapter 2

# Why So Many?

## Types of Credit

## Credit Cards and Their Use

Credit cards are a form of loan made usually by a bank, merchant, gasoline company, department store, or credit card company. The cost of that type of credit is considerably higher than for a personal loan at a bank or a savings and loan association. The interest rates are high (some up to 22 percent). Depending on the type of credit card you have, an annual fee may be charged. Some companies assess fees for late payments or increase your interest rate if you are late in making a payment.

Some banks offer credit cards without charging an annual fee, but they usually have a high interest rate or no grace period in making payments. The grace period or "float" is a period of time before interest is charged on outstanding balances, usually 25 to 30 days. By paying the full balance at the end of the month, you will avoid paying interest.

So-called teaser credit cards offer low interest rates initially and then adjust to higher rates. And some credit card companies offer incentives—for example, rebates or frequent flyer miles.

The companies that provide credit to consumers also make money by charging merchants (and service providers) a fee each time a consumer uses a company's credit card in the merchant's place of business. Each time a customer uses his or her credit card, the merchant pays to the issuing credit card company a small percentage of the amount the customer charged. You can imagine that with the millions of holders using their credit cards, credit card companies make huge profits.

There are five different types of plastic credit cards, three of which are used for credit purchases. All five cards have different functions. You need to read your contractual agreement before using any of these cards for information about annual fees, interest rates, and credit limits. The information provides guidance on using the cards.

## Bank Cards

Visa and MasterCard cards are issued by a bank or other institution that has a contract with the Visa or the MasterCard organization. The banks offering Visa or MasterCard are competitive with their rates and terms, which is why it's important to shop around at several banks or institutions before sending in an application. A few, but not many, banks or institutions do not charge an annual fee. Some interest rates are as low as 6.9 percent, while some are as high as 22 percent. With a bank card you may take a cash advance against your credit limit, but be prepared to be assessed 3 to 4 percent of the cash advance, and usually there's no grace period on cash advances.

Gold cards, sometimes referred to as premium cards, have higher credit limits that can range from $5,000 to $50,000. The annual fees are higher and the qualifications much more difficult.

Visa and MasterCard cards are considered major credit cards and are probably the most widely accepted. In most stores Visa and MasterCard cards can be used in place of a store's charge card. They can also be used in most restaurants and hotels. Any business establishment that is a member of the Visa or MasterCard network can accept the appropriate card. It is, in other words, a universal charge card.

## Seller Credit Cards

Seller credit cards are known as business charge account cards and are issued by department, tire, furniture, jewelry, and appliance stores. Oil and gasoline companies have their own charge cards as do airline and car rental companies, all of whom use charge cards to increase their business. Those types of charge accounts are limited to the company that issued the card.

An annual fee is seldom charged on seller accounts, although the interest rates are usually high. Billing statements and payment procedures are similar to those accompanying bank credit cards.

## Travel and Entertainment Cards

Credit cards issued by American Express, Diners Club, and Carte Blanche are known as travel and entertainment cards; they have an annual fee and require a payment in full each month. Whatever you have charged appears on your monthly statement and must be paid by the due date shown on the statement. There are no finance privileges or cash advances. If you don't pay the full amount by the due date, a one-month grace period is allowed without an interest charge. If no payment is made by the end of the grace period, the company will begin to charge you interest. After three months without payment, it will probably close out your account. Interest is then charged monthly until the bill is paid.

American Express has three types of travel and entertainment cards: the green card, the gold card, and the platinum card. Each card has its own credit limit, and annual fees differ with each card.

The charge card company makes its profit by charging large annual fees. The fees they charge merchants when customers pay through their card are higher than fees associated with bank cards.

Travel and entertainment cards have more stringent credit requirements and terms than bank cards because their balances have to be paid in full at the end of each billing period.

## ATM Cards

Automated Teller Machine (ATM) cards are issued by banks and by savings and loan associations (S&Ls). Introduced to give banking customers flexibility in banking hours, ATM machines are open 24 hours a day.

By using your ATM card at the bank or branch where you have an account, you can withdraw money, make deposits, transfer money between accounts, find out your balance, and make loan payments. You can use another bank's ATM machine (other than your own) to withdraw cash or find out your balance, but if you do, you may be charged a service fee. Deposits or payments cannot be made in another bank's ATM machine.

## Debit Cards

Debit cards are issued by banks and combine the functions of ATM cards and checks. The most common places to see transactions with a debit card are at grocery stores or oil and gasoline stations. Department stores may follow this trend in the near future.

Many banks are now offering debit cards that look like a Visa or MasterCard card, but they work like a check, subtracting money from your checking account within days, or minutes, of your transaction. You can use a debit card with a personal identification number (PIN) to get cash at your bank machine or pay for purchases at stores that handle such transactions. You can use it as you would a credit card; a sales clerk in fact wouldn't know the difference. Be sure and keep track of purchases you make with your debit card.

**Credit cards versus debit cards.**   A debit card is similar to a credit card except that any amounts charged on the card are immediately deducted from the cardholder's checking or savings account. No interest is charged; only the amount of a charged purchase is deducted from your bank account.

Debit cards are becoming more popular with consumers for their convenience. When using your debit card, it is important to deduct in your checkbook the amount charged so you keep a proper balance.

A credit card, on the other hand, creates a bill; the debit card automatically pays a bill. An ATM or debit card is issued by your bank, whereas a credit card has no connection with your bank accounts.

Credit cards offer three important advantages over debit cards:

1. You get a float with a credit card because your account is not immediately debited. If you charge with a credit card, for example, you would have approximately 25 to 30 days to pay the charge. Most banks charge no interest if paid within the grace period. With a debit card your account registers a deduction immediately.
2. A credit card allows more leverage in settling disputes about purchases made.
3. The liability is less with a credit card that is lost or stolen than with a debit card.

Because debit cards are often substituted for cash, they are more often compared with checks than with credit cards. To use your debit card, the proper equipment that can electronically transmit the information on your card to the bank must be available. The proper equipment also credits the account of the merchant where your purchase was made with the amount of the sale.

## Credit Card Worksheet

Make a list of your current cards.

1. Travel and Entertainment Cards

_____

_____

_____

_____

2. Charge Cards

_____

_____

_____

_____

3. Bank Cards

_____

_____

_____

_____

4. ATM and Debit Cards

_____

_____

_____

_____

## Credit Cards Desired Worksheet

1. Travel and Entertainment Cards

_____

_____

_____

_____

2. Charge Cards

_____

_____

_____

_____

3. Bank Cards

_____

_____

_____

_____

4. ATM and Debit Cards

_____

_____

_____

_____

## Preferred Credit Cards

A *preferred credit card* is one that is issued after you fill out an application with the desired creditor and are approved. It is usually issued by Visa and/or MasterCard. After reviewing the application and completing a credit check, the creditor will issue a card to an applicant if all the criteria are met. The institution extending the credit card sets a limit on the card, which allows the cardholder to charge up to the designated limit. That kind of card is known as an *unsecured card,* or a preferred credit card. No money deposit is required to obtain a preferred card.

Payment on a preferred credit card must be made monthly according to the terms of the contract. Pay your account before the due date to set up a good payment pattern, and do not exceed your credit limit. The creditor reports your monthly activity to the one or more credit reporting agencies to which it subscribes. Creditors subscribe to specific credit reporting bureaus—for example, Experian (formerly TRW), Trans Union, and Equifax.

To increase your line of credit, you need a good payment history for at least three to six months. A creditor will review your account when you request an increase. Every creditor has a different policy, but, generally, all creditors will probably grant a request for an increase in your credit limit if they see a good payment pattern. One way to qualify for a credit limit increase is to pay more than the minimum amount you owe. For example, if the minimum due is $40, pay $80 on the account before the due date. That kind of payment record will increase your chances of a credit increase. *Do not* go over your credit limit, which can cost you the renewal of your credit card. If you run over the limit occasionally, be sure to pay it down as soon as possible.

Be sure to know your interest rates and annual fees. Refer ahead to Chapter 4 on applying for credit.

The best suggestion is to not use your credit cards unless you plan on paying the whole balance off at the end of the month. Your credit cards should be used for the following:

- Building a good credit history
- Emergencies with the intention to repay immediately
- To make money

There are many nationwide banks throughout the United States from which you can request credit applications. Be sure to check requirements before applying for credit cards from the nationwide banks and S&Ls listed below:

- Citibank (800-843-0777)
- Chase Manhattan (800-441-7683)
- First Card (800-368-4535)
- MBNA (800-847-7378)
- Chase Bank (800-648-3355)

## Credit Card Information Worksheet

List all your credit cards that are unsecured. Include the annual fee and the annual percentage rate.

| Credit Card Company | Annual Fee | Annual Percentage Rate |
|---|---|---|
| | | |
| | | |
| | | |
| | | |
| | | |
| | | |
| | | |
| | | |
| | | |

- Household Credit Services (800-477-6000)
- First USA Bank (800-955-9900)

Get in touch with Bankcard Holders of America to receive a list of banks and institutions offering gold credit card applications. Gold cards have a higher credit limit than other cards—usually $5,000 and above—and the annual fees are usually higher. Bankcard Holders also provides lists of banks and institutions offering credit cards with low interest rates and those offering no annual fees. To get more information call Bankcard Holders of America at 540-389-5445.

## Secured Credit Cards

The guaranteed credit card, also known as a *secured credit card,* can be issued by either Visa or MasterCard. The secured Visa and MasterCard programs are set up differently than preferred credit card programs. Advertisements that read "Get Visa®/MasterCard®: No credit, bad credit, bankruptcies, guaranteed approval" are for secured Visa or MasterCard credit cards. Some consumers have had bad luck in their past—unemployment, divorce, illness, hospitalization—when bills became delinquent and were placed with collection companies or charged off. Many people have experienced repossessions, judgments, tax liens, or were forced to file for bankruptcy. All of those negative actions appear on an individual's credit report, preventing them from getting new credit. Or an individual may have no credit history, which is almost as severe as having bad credit. Without any credit, no payment pattern is established on credit reports and will result in a credit denial. In all such situations a secured credit card is beneficial.

## *Terms*

To qualify for a secured credit card a consumer must open a savings account with a designated bank. A deposit, which the bank will specify, must be made. Each bank sets the amount required; it could range from $300 to $5,000. The bank in return will issue the customer a Visa or MasterCard credit card, securing it with the full amount of the deposit or a percentage of the amount deposited. For example, if you deposit $300, your credit limit is $300; or if you deposit $1,000, and the bank allows you to charge only up to 50 percent of your balance, your credit limit is $500. Each bank is different and will notify you of its requirements prior to your deposit.

The banks that offer secured credit cards pay you interest on your deposit; however, they also charge interest for use of your card to make purchases, and some banks charge a yearly fee for a secured credit card.

Most of the banks that offer secured credit cards charge a one-time processing fee with the initial application that can range from $35 to $65 per card. Once the application is approved, an annual fee is charged and appears on your credit card once a year.

## *Questions to Ask*

Once your card is approved, make sure you are aware of the bank's policies. Before you make a deposit, make sure you know the answers to the following questions:

- What is the annual fee?
- How much is the required deposit?
- How much of the deposit can be used to charge purchases?

- What interest rate does the bank pay on the deposit?
- How much interest is charged for purchases made with the credit card?

*Do not give your money to anyone other than the bank!* Verify that this is not a scam and that there really is a bank offering this program.

Most of the banks offering secured credit cards will be out of your state, so be sure to send your deposit by registered mail with a return receipt requested.

Because a secured card looks no different than a preferred card, almost no one is able to tell the difference between the two. Approximately 90 to 95 percent of the people applying for a secured card are approved. The bank's protection is the deposit. Not being approved is usually the result of an incomplete application.

The payments you make on your secured credit card show up on your credit report, which is why you can use your secured card to establish new credit and also establish a good credit background if you've had past credit problems.

A secured credit card account can be closed at any time if all charges have been paid. After you establish a good track record and your credit report improves, then apply for a preferred card.

There are some new banks offering unsecured credit cards to individuals with past credit problems. Contact Professional Credit Counselors for more details (1100 Irvine Blvd., #541, Tustin, CA 92780, 714-541-2637).

## Be Cautious

A word of caution when reading advertisements for a secured credit card. Make sure the name of the bank that is offering it is in the ad or the application. Call the bank directly to make sure it really exists before submitting the application. Find out if it has any outside customer service assisting it. Call the better business bureau to see if there have been any complaints about the bank.

Banks that offer secured credit cards are difficult to find. The list is small, but check with your own bank to see if it offers a secured card. Following are some that do:

## Sample Letter to Request Secured Credit Cards

---

XYZ Bank
1111 Main St.
Anytown, CA 00002

To Whom It May Concern:

Please send me an application for your secured Visa and MasterCard cards. What is your annual fee? What interest do you pay? What is your annual percentage rate?

Thank you.

John Doe
2299 Sycamore
Anytown, NY 55551

- Key Bank and Trust (800-539-5398)
- Orchard Bank (800-873-7307)
- Dreyfus Thrift & Commerce (800-727-3348)
- Spirit Visa (800-779-8472)
- First Consumers National Bank (800-876-3262)
- Bank One Arizona (800-544-4110)

## Unsolicited Credit and Charge Cards

Many companies are eager to issue credit cards and often solicit new accounts by sending preapproved credit card applications to individuals. If a company wants to do this, it can legally send you a letter stating that you have been prequalified for a certain line of credit. The application is a simple form that usually requires little more than a signature.

## Secured Credit Card Worksheet

When applying and obtaining secured credit cards, list the following:

Name of institution _____

Visa or MasterCard _____

Minimum deposit _____

Annual fee _____

Interest rate charged _____

Interest paid by bank on deposit _____

Name of institution _____

Visa or MasterCard _____

Minimum deposit _____

Annual fee _____

Interest rate charged _____

Interest paid by bank on deposit _____

Name of institution _____

Visa or MasterCard _____

Minimum deposit _____

Annual fee _____

Interest rate charged _____

Interest paid by bank on deposit _____

## Use Caution before Signing

By signing the form sent by the credit card company, you are agreeing to its terms. You are also authorizing the company to check your credit report as well as report to the credit bureaus any activity you have with the company. Frequently the lines of credit that are set with that type of preapproved credit card are low to protect the company in case of problems. The credit lines may be increased later to a higher limit.

Any application or solicitation by a credit card company must state the following:

- The monthly finance charge
- The yearly interest rate that is known as the annual percentage rate (the monthly finance charge multiplied by 12)
- The annual yearly fee
- The range of balances
- Fixed or variable interest
- The number of days you're allowed to pay off the entire balance without an interest charge, known as the grace period (If this does not apply, when the interest charge begins must be stated.)
- Any charges for cash advances, late charges, over-the-limit fees, or for returned checks

Once you receive your credit card and do not return it, all credit activity will begin.

## Do Not Throw It Away

If you receive a preapproved credit card and decide that you don't want it, do not throw it away. By throwing it away, you are not letting the company know that you will not be using it. Your credit file will show that you have an active account that is reported to the credit reporting bureaus. This indicates that you have an active line of credit and could hurt your chances of obtaining new credit or any credit line increases. Creditors do not want to see too much credit on a credit report.

Instead of throwing these credit cards away, cut them up and return them to the credit card issuer with a letter stating that you don't want the card or the account opened. Send your letter certified mail with a return receipt requested to avoid a credit entry. And do the same for a card you don't want to renew. After you have sent your letter, wait three weeks and then request a copy of your credit report from a credit bureau. Check your credit report to make sure no entry was reported.

One of my clients received an unsolicited credit card. She didn't want the card and threw it in the trash. She began receiving statements for the annual fee and disregarded the statements.

After receiving a copy of her credit report, she discovered the credit card company had placed a negative entry on her report for nonpayment.

## Sample Letter Rejecting a Preapproved Credit Card

May 1, 19___
Incon Card Services
77891 First St.
Maintown, State, Zip

Account number: 00019892039

Dear Consumer Service Dept,

I have cut up my credit card and am returning it with this letter. I do not wish to open an account with your company. Please cancel my account immediately.

Sincerely,

Dave Dolstrom

She explained to the company that she had thrown the card away, but they still demanded payment of the fee. Because she had not written the company to cancel the account and had not returned the credit card directly to the company, the company would not waive the fee.

## Instant Credit

Many people today do not realize that they may be eligible to receive instant credit. Many department stores, jewelry stores, tire stores, and other merchants offer instant credit. If you have an American Express, Visa, or MasterCard card, credit will be extended almost immediately. Once you complete the application, the store will issue you a temporary credit card to use in the store for that particular day. The application will be called into the store's main branch and a credit check done at that time. Once the credit report is completed, sometimes within 30 minutes, you will be given a line of credit and your permanent card mailed within two to four weeks.

### You May Be Denied

If there is a problem with your credit application or credit report, a store may decline your application for instant credit. The decline may not come for several days. Should that happen, the card which you used for the day of application will be good only for that particular day. If you are denied the credit card and have made any purchases, you will be billed monthly for the balance.

Should a denial occur, the store must notify you in writing and indicate which credit agency it used. Once you know which credit agency was used, you are entitled to a free credit report if you submit a request within 30 days of the denial.

### Pay the Payments Anyway

Make the monthly payments on the bill before they are due because your debt will be reported on your credit report even if you have been denied credit. The denial does not show up on the credit report. Because you're trying to build up a good payment pattern, it is better if you don't eliminate the entire balance in one payment unless the creditor requests it. Pay monthly as indicated on each statement so that a good payment record will appear on your credit report.

## Lines of Credit

The two different lines of credit are secured and unsecured.

### Secured Credit

*Secured* credit refers to your purchase of an item under a contractual agreement indicating a specific item or items as collateral. The collateral guarantees that you will make the payments. If you don't, the creditor is entitled to take the designated item or items back. For example, if you have purchased an automobile and don't make the payments, the company that made the loan can repossess the car. The loan company's security is the car. It may sell the car, but if it collects less than the amount you owe, the company can bring a lawsuit against you to collect the difference between the price you paid for the car and the amount of the loan.

## Secured Credit Worksheet

List the items you have that are secured and the companies from which you obtained them.

**Company Name**                                                    **Item**

_____

_____

_____

_____

_____

_____

_____

_____

Whenever you take out a secured loan, in most cases the loan company will have you sign a *security agreement* that specifies what items or property can be taken should you default. According to the security agreement, the creditor has a legal right to take possession of the item pledged as security if you do not pay.

There are two types of security agreements: A *purchase money agreement* is a pledge of the property you are actually buying, such as furniture, appliances, and motor vehicles. A *nonpurchase money agreement* is a pledge of certain property as security for the money you have borrowed.

**Examples of secured credit.** Some common examples of secured debts include the following:

- A mortgage to buy or refinance a home or other real estate is a secured debt. The security or collateral is the property. If you stop making payments, the mortgage company can foreclose on the property—that is, the property reverts back to the lender and you lose the title.

- Loans for cars, boats, and recreational vehicles are secured by the vehicles themselves. If you fail to pay, the vehicles will be taken back by the loan company.
- Stores that carry furniture or major appliances usually require a signed security agreement. The item you purchase is the collateral for repayment so that if you fail to pay, the item will be taken back. Some stores, on the other hand, allow customers to charge furniture or appliances with an unsecured credit card.
- Finance companies, which offer personal loans, will ask for your personal property as collateral and could include automobiles or furniture that are paid off. Anything of value can be included as collateral.
- Secured credit cards are secured by the amount of the deposit you have with the issuing bank.

## Unsecured Credit

*Unsecured credit* is credit that is established with no collateral. Most of the debts that individuals incur, in fact, are unsecured. The majority of credit card companies offer unsecured credit cards that are used for purchasing merchandise. If you stop making payments on credit card purchases, the purchases cannot be repossessed. The only option a store has for collecting an unpaid debt is to sue you and get a court judgment for the amount you owe.

Unsecured credit is not limited to credit cards. Following are numerous examples of unsecured debt:

- Utility bills (telephone, gas, electric, water, and cable)
- Medical bills (doctors, dentists, and chiropractors)
- Loans from friends and relatives
- Rent
- Gasoline and most department store charges
- Credit and charge card purchases
- Newspaper and magazine subscriptions
- Accountant fees
- Attorney fees
- Child support and alimony
- Student loans

---

### Unsecured Credit Worksheet

List the companies where you have unsecured credit.

**Company Name**                                                    **Item**

_____

_____

_____

_____

_____

_____

_____

_____

_____

_____

_____

---

## Protecting Your Credit

### Credit Card Payments

Have you ever read an ad or heard an advertisement that states "No payment for six months with purchase"? This type of advertisement may entice you to make a purchase because you don't have to make any payments for six months. BEWARE! READ THE SMALL PRINT.

### Deferred Payments

Deferment for six months of a payment is fine so long as you are not being charged interest for those six months, but many deferment plans add interest to your loan on a monthly basis. For example, if you now have a $450 balance due and then make a purchase of $250, your new balance will be $700. The $250 will not be added to your balance due now, but the interest or finance charge on the $250 will be added monthly, which will increase your balance. Six months later, when your first payment on the $250 begins, six months' interest has been added to your balance.

Not all companies do this. Some will not charge any interest or assess finance charges during the indicated time, which is to your advantage. Your balance won't increase and you can have those six months (or whatever the time period was) to pay off the amount you owe.

Purchasing with credit cards or charge cards of companies that offer deferred programs should encourage consumers to purchase wisely. Deferred programs make it easy for consumers to buy things they really don't need. The only advantage is to give them additional time to pay off purchases. But don't fall into the trap of a deferred payment plan in which interest is charged during the deferment period.

Make sure you understand the contract and type of deferment plan you are getting into. This will make you a wise shopper.

## Credit Card Payments

The billing cycle for most credit cards is 25 to 30 days. It is wise to make your credit card payments within that time frame. Frequently the due date on the statement will also have a billing date. If the payment is received by the billing date, it is not considered delinquent by most companies. Once a new billing date appears and a payment has not been received, the account becomes delinquent.

If you missed the billing date, make your payment as soon as possible. Most creditors don't report a delinquency to a credit reporting agency until you are two payments late. A late payment appears only in a creditor's internal system if you are delinquent the first month.

Do not lump two payments into one. It is important to keep them separated so that your payment pattern doesn't show a skipped payment. Make the payments separately even if they are spaced one day apart.

Contact your creditor and ask how many days you can be delinquent before the delinquency is reported to the credit reporting agency.

## Important Facts about Credit Cards

1. Keep credit cards in a safe place; for example, a safe deposit box.
2. Sign your credit card immediately upon receiving it.
3. Notify creditors of any address change.
4. If credit cards are stolen, notify creditors immediately.
5. Upon receipt of your credit card statement, reconcile all purchases.
6. Pay off the balances you owe before the bill is due.
7. Keep all pertinent information about your credit cards in a safe place; include the name of each creditor, its address and phone number, your account number, and the card's expiration date. This information is necessary in case of theft or loss. (Complete the Credit Card Information Worksheet.)
8. Never sign a blank receipt; always total the receipt.
9. Save your receipts to assist you in reconciling statements.
10. Destroy carbons.
11. Never lend your card to anyone.
12. Do not give your credit card number over the phone unless you are confident the company is legitimate.
13. Do not carry your PIN number with your credit card for cash withdrawals at ATM machines.

## Ten Commandments of Credit

1. Thou shall not overextend thy card.
2. Thou shall not be a compulsive charge addict.
3. Know thy credit report.
4. Know thy legal rights.
5. Thou shall not sign a blank charge slip.
6. Know thy account numbers and creditors' names and addresses.
7. Respect thy creditors when you have a problem.
8. Thou shall review all charge statements.
9. Thou shall pay bills promptly.
10. Thou shall destroy all carbons from charge slips.

# Credit Card Information Worksheet

Make a list of all your credit cards with the following information.

Creditor's name _____

Address _____ Telephone _____

Account number_____

Expiration date _____ Interest rate _____ Credit limit _____

Creditor's name _____

Address _____ Telephone _____

Account number_____

Expiration date _____ Interest rate _____ Credit limit _____

Creditor's name _____

Address _____ Telephone _____

Account number_____

Expiration date _____ Interest rate _____ Credit limit _____

Creditor's name _____

Address _____ Telephone _____

Account number_____

Expiration date _____ Interest rate _____ Credit limit _____

# Chapter 3

# I Thought I Was Out of School!

## Qualifying for Credit

When applying for credit, you have to know what credit grantors are looking for before they will grant you a line of credit. When granting credit by means of a credit card, a mortgage, a car, or a loan, creditors look for an ability to repay the debt and a willingness to do so. Creditors, in other words, are looking for the three "Cs" of credit: *capacity, character,* and *collateral.*

## The Three Cs of Credit

**Capacity.** The creditor wants to make sure you can repay the debt. To qualify you on the initial application, there are questions about your current employment, including the length of time you have been employed. Creditors want to know what your income is and any bonuses you may receive. They want to know what and how much your expenses are, how many dependents you have, and if you are paying child support and/or alimony.

One of the most important features about capacity is the debt to income ratio. Debt to income is calculated by totaling all your monthly debt (for example, car payments, rent or mortgage, credit card payments, alimony, child support), including the monthly payment for the item you are trying to finance, and then dividing this total by your monthly

## Debt to Income Calculation Worksheet

| Gross Monthly Income | | Monthly Fixed Income | |
|---|---|---|---|
| Salary | $_____ | Rent or mortgage | $_____ |
| Spouse's salary | _____ | Automobile | _____ |
| Commissions | _____ | Automobile | _____ |
| Bonuses | _____ | Bank installments | _____ |
| Alimony | _____ | Charge/Revolving acc'ts | _____ |
| Child Support | _____ | Child support | _____ |
| Other | _____ | Alimony | _____ |
| Total income | $_____ | Other | _____ |
| (Before taxes) | _____ | Other | _____ |
| | | Proposed loan payment | |
| | | Total payments | $_____ |

The total monthly payments _____ divided by the total monthly gross income _____ equals your debt ratio _____ . If the ratio is over 50 percent, the banks may not approve the loan. Contact the lending institution before you apply for any credit to determine what its loan to debt ratio policies are.

income. Most banks will not lend you money if the ratio is over 50 percent. You need to ask the credit grantor before you apply for credit what its acceptable ratio is (see Debt to Income Calculation Worksheet).

**Character.** Creditors will look at your credit history and your paying habits, from information they get through a credit reporting agency such as Experian, Trans Union, or Equifax. They are looking for stability and thus will look at the length of time you've lived at your current address and whether you own or rent your home.

**Collateral.**  Creditors want to know if they are protected should you stop paying on the loan or debt. Showing what assets you have, other than income from your job, can put a creditor's mind at ease. Assets could be a savings account, investments, or property—any or all of which a credit grantor will consider security for the loan because they can be liquidated if you fall into financial difficulties.

It is important that you excel in all three areas to increase your chances of an approval. Moreover, you need to know where your strengths and weaknesses are before you apply for credit (see Strength and Weaknesses Worksheet).

# Credit Criteria

The following criteria are reviewed carefully by credit grantors before they will approve a loan application:

## Employment.

* How long have you been at your current job?
* How long have you been in the same line of work?
* Are you self-employed?
* How much is your income?
* Are you paid on commission only?

Answers to the above questions indicate your character and capacity to repay the loan or establish credit. If you have been employed for less than a year or show irregular employment, the application will most likely be rejected. If your income is irregular or unstable, your application will also be rejected.

## Previous credit.

* Do you have credit now?
* Have you established credit in the past?
* Have you paid your monthly obligations satisfactorily?

Credit grantors will look at your past payment patterns by obtaining a copy of your credit report. They will be able to see what obligations you presently have and if the accounts were paid satisfactorily. Most credit grantors feel that if you paid your past obligations on time,

## Strengths and Weaknesses Worksheet

Before filling out a credit application, you need to know where your strengths and weaknesses lie. Answer each of the following questions.

1. How long have you been employed at your current job?

   _____

2. How long have you been in the same line of work?

   _____

3. Are you self-employed?

   _____

4. How much is your income?

   _____

5. Are you paid on commission only?

   _____

6. Do you have credit now?

   _____

7. Have you established credit in the past?

   _____

8. Have you paid your monthly obligations satisfactorily?

   _____

9. Do you own or rent your home?

   _____

10. Do you have a checking and/or savings account? List.

    _____

11. What debts do you owe at the present time?

    _____

you will continue the same pattern. But if you were negligent and irresponsible with your past credit, you will probably follow the same pattern. Problems, however, that prevent you from making your payments can arise, so occasionally an explanation of your past problems and how you corrected them is all a credit grantor needs to know to approve an application. If your credit history is poor and unclear, you will be rejected.

## Residency.

- Do you own or rent your home?

If you own your home, lenders will feel more comfortable with your application, knowing there is more stability. It would be hard to run away if there ever is a problem. Also, equity has built up in your home if you ever need to sell it or use it for obtaining cash.

If you are renting, then credit grantors will look at how long you have been at the residence. They will also want to know how long you were at your previous address. The key is once again stability. You have a high chance of rejection if you've been at your present address less than a year.

## Checking and savings accounts.

- Do you have a checking or savings account?

Creditors want to know that you have money in a checking account for writing checks and covering your payments.

By having a savings account, you assure credit grantors that you're able to save money and have money set aside for emergencies.

## Open accounts.

- What debts do you owe at the present time?

If you are current on all your outstanding accounts, credit grantors will view your application favorably because you've shown both responsibility and an ability to repay a loan.

## *Complete and Accurate Application*

All information you complete on your credit application will be compared with your credit report. Creditors will reject an applicant for information that appears on a credit report but is not included in the initial application.

Be sure that all the information on the credit application is verifiable and correct. If you provide information that is incorrect or falsified in any way, the credit application will be rejected. If, after approving your application, a grantor found that the information you provided was fraudulent, the credit grantor could sue you.

## Credit Scoring

Creditors use different combinations of the facts reviewed above in reaching a decision. They also use different kinds of rating systems, some relying on their instincts and others using a "credit scoring" system. In a scoring system, a certain number of points are assigned to each of the various characteristics and points are awarded for each factor that the creditor considers important. Creditors generally offer credit to consumers awarded the most points because the scoring has proved to be a reliable method for evaluating a borrower's likelihood of repaying the debt (see Credit Scoring Worksheet).

Each credit grantor has different criteria. Call or write before applying for a credit card or loan to see what each creditor's priorities are.

For scores that total more than 18 points, there is a good chance the application will be approved.

The sample credit scoring is to be used as a guideline only and does not guarantee approval on any bank or savings and loan application.

## Credit Scoring Sample

Review these categories; then turn to the Credit Scoring Worksheet.

### Marital Status

Married . . . . . . . . . . . . . . . 2
Single . . . . . . . . . . . . . . . 1

### Age

18-25 . . . . . . . . . . . . . . . . 0
26-65 . . . . . . . . . . . . . . . . 1
66+ . . . . . . . . . . . . . . . . . 0

### Dependents

One . . . . . . . . . . . . . . . . . 2
Two . . . . . . . . . . . . . . . . . 2
Three . . . . . . . . . . . . . . . . 3
Four . . . . . . . . . . . . . . . . . 1
Five . . . . . . . . . . . . . . . . . 0

### Current Residence

Less than 2 yrs . . . . . . . . . . 1
2-3 yrs . . . . . . . . . . . . . . . 2
4-6 yrs . . . . . . . . . . . . . . . 3
Over 6 yrs . . . . . . . . . . . 4

### Residence

Own, no payment . . . . . . . 4
Own, mortgage . . . . . . . . . 3
Rent, unfurnished . . . . . . . 2
Any other . . . . . . . . . . . . . 0

### Previous Residence

0-3 yrs . . . . . . . . . . . . . . . 1
3-6 yrs . . . . . . . . . . . . . . . 2

### Employment

Less than 1yr . . . . . . . . . . 0
1-3 yrs . . . . . . . . . . . . . . 1
3-6 yrs . . . . . . . . . . . . . . 2
6 yrs+ . . . . . . . . . . . . . . . 3

### Occupation

Unskilled . . . . . . . . . . . . . 1
Skilled . . . . . . . . . . . . . . . 2
Professional . . . . . . . . . . . 3

### Credit History

Loan at bank
where applied . . . . . . . . 4
Loan at another bank . . . . . 3

### Monthly Income

Up to $600 . . . . . . . . . . . . 1

$600 to $800 . . . . . . . . . . . 2
$800 to $1,000 . . . . . . . . . 3
$1,000+ . . . . . . . . . . . . . . 5

### Monthly Obligations

$0 to $250 . . . . . . . . . . . . 1
$259+ . . . . . . . . . . . . . . . 0

### Additional

Phone listed . . . . . . . . . . . 2
Phone unlisted . . . . . . . . . 0
Checking or savings
account . . . . . . . . . . . . 2

# Credit Scoring Worksheet

| **Marital Status** | **Age** |
|---|---|
| Married . . . . . . . . . . . . . . . . . . . . . | 18–25 . . . . . . . . . . . . . . . . . . . . . . . |
| Single . . . . . . . . . . . . . . . . . . . . . . | 26–65 . . . . . . . . . . . . . . . . . . . . . . . |
| | 66+ . . . . . . . . . . . . . . . . . . . . . . . . |

| **Dependents** | **Current Residence** |
|---|---|
| One . . . . . . . . . . . . . . . . . . . . . . . . | Less than 2 yrs . . . . . . . . . . . . . . . . |
| Two. . . . . . . . . . . . . . . . . . . . . . . . | 2–3 yrs . . . . . . . . . . . . . . . . . . . . . |
| Three. . . . . . . . . . . . . . . . . . . . . . . | 4–6 yrs . . . . . . . . . . . . . . . . . . . . . |
| Four. . . . . . . . . . . . . . . . . . . . . . . . | Over 6 yrs. . . . . . . . . . . . . . . . . . . . |
| Five . . . . . . . . . . . . . . . . . . . . . . . | |

| **Residence** | **Previous Residence** |
|---|---|
| Own, no payment. . . . . . . . . . . . . | 0–3 yrs . . . . . . . . . . . . . . . . . . . . . |
| Own, mortgage. . . . . . . . . . . . . . . | 3–6 yrs . . . . . . . . . . . . . . . . . . . . . |
| Rent, unfurnished. . . . . . . . . . . . . | |
| Any other . . . . . . . . . . . . . . . . . . . | |

| **Employment** | **Occupation** |
|---|---|
| Less than 1yr. . . . . . . . . . . . . . . . . | Unskilled . . . . . . . . . . . . . . . . . . . . |
| 1–3 yrs . . . . . . . . . . . . . . . . . . . . . | Skilled. . . . . . . . . . . . . . . . . . . . . . |
| 3–6 yrs . . . . . . . . . . . . . . . . . . . . . | Professional . . . . . . . . . . . . . . . . . . |
| 6 yrs+. . . . . . . . . . . . . . . . . . . . . . | |

| **Credit History** | **Monthly Income** |
|---|---|
| Loan at bank where applied . . . . . . | Up to $600 . . . . . . . . . . . . . . . . . . |
| Loan at another bank . . . . . . . . . . | $600 to $800 . . . . . . . . . . . . . . . . . |
| | $800 to $1,000. . . . . . . . . . . . . . . . |
| | $1,000+. . . . . . . . . . . . . . . . . . . . . |

| **Monthly Obligations** | **Additional** |
|---|---|
| $0 to $250. . . . . . . . . . . . . . . . . . | Phone listed . . . . . . . . . . . . . . . . . . |
| $259+ . . . . . . . . . . . . . . . . . . . . . | Phone unlisted . . . . . . . . . . . . . . . . |
| | Checking or savings account . . . . . |

## Who Qualifies for Credit?

Creditors are always looking for potential credit card applicants who are 18 years old or older. Certain requirements must be met, however, by everyone to be approved for a credit card. Listed below are various groups that will qualify for credit.

**High school students.** A high school student who is 18 years old may receive an application for a credit card. In most cases an 18-year-old is a senior in high school and almost ready to graduate. A typical letter of enticement to a student would be:

Dear Christen,

XYZ Bank is ready to help you take a big step into the future with a credit card just for you. The card has a credit limit of up to $500. It gives you the security of knowing that you are ready for anything. It may be a last-minute purchase as you leave for college or start your career. If an emergency arises, you have a credit card to help with whatever expenses arise.

Simply fill out the Acceptance Certificate, have your parent or guardian fill out the Guarantor Section, and you are on your way to having your very own credit card.

You would be surprised at how many ways a credit card can help you. It can be used for identification and for getting cash when you need it.

Most important, it is the first step to building a strong credit history for your future. The careful use of your credit card will show that you are ready to handle more responsibility.

You do not have to be currently employed because being a student is a full-time job. Nor is a previous credit history required for students.

Complete the short Acceptance Certificate, and we will process your application immediately.

Sincerely,

William Brown
Executive Vice President

The short Acceptance Certificate will typically have the pertinent information needed for a young adult: name, address, Social Security number, year of birth, and college/university or employer.

The second portion of the Acceptance Certificate is for the parent or guardian to complete. It is the Guarantor Section in which a parent or guardian guarantees the line of credit and thus becomes a cosigner for the young adult. If the young adult fails to make any payments, the parent or guardian is responsible.

The information in the guarantor's section to be completed usually includes the guarantor's full name, address, Social Security number, home telephone number, business telephone number, employer, and gross monthly income.

An accompanying section would probably state the following:

Please read carefully: I hereby apply to XYZ Bank for a credit card. I have read the important disclosures and miscellaneous information, and agree to be bound as specified therein. Both signatures are required. I authorize XYZ Bank to verify my employment. $15,000 minimum annual household income required.

The important disclosures and miscellaneous information include the interest rate, annual fee, grace period for repayment, method of computing the balance for purchases, and fees for cash advances, late payment, and going over the credit limit. The miscellaneous information includes giving the company authorization to check and exchange credit information on the applicant and list any state regulations that pertain to the credit card company.

The important thing is that many applications for credit for a young adult or student will require a cosigner. Some companies will issue credit cards to a young adult without a cosigner providing the young adult is a full-time student, but the credit limit would be minimal.

**College students.** College students may apply for credit cards, and because they are full-time students, many credit card companies will give them credit. The application procedures are similar to those for high school students, as previously discussed. In the application it is necessary to indicate the name of the college or university attended with some type of proof such as a statement from the school or a report card. The credit limit would be minimal, and a cosigner is not usually required.

**Employed individuals.** If you have been employed for a minimum of one to two years, you have a good chance of qualifying for a line of credit or a credit card. Frequently, an amount for qualifying is stated on the credit application. For example, it may say "Applicant must have a $12,000 gross income per year to apply." This must be verifiable to the creditor should it call or write your employer.

The higher your income, the higher the line of credit granted. The creditor is looking for stability. Besides stable employment, the credit grantor will also look at your reported credit history and length of time you've lived at your current residence. All factors are taken into consideration to determine credit eligibility (refer to the Credit Scoring Worksheet in a previous section).

**Unemployed individuals.** Creditors are looking for job stability, so if you are unemployed, it is best not to apply for a line of credit or a credit card. The risk for the credit grantor is just too high.

If you've been employed but have been laid off and remain unemployed, the credit that has already been established will not be affected providing your accounts do not become delinquent. If they do become delinquent, the creditor may cancel your account. When a creditor feels a debtor poses a high risk of not making payments, the creditor may cancel the account. If the situation appears to be temporary, however, a creditor will probably work out a repayment plan.

**Self-employed individuals.** The self-employed have a harder time qualifying for credit than those who have an employer. A self-employed worker is usually expected to have been self-employed for a minimum of two years to be eligible for credit approval. The best way for the self-employed to show that creditors' risk is minimal is to provide photocopies of two years of tax returns or a 1099 form along with the credit application to verify their business income.

In addition to an applicant's verifications of income, creditors will also review the applicant's credit report and other pertinent factors. If the credit scoring is high enough, a line of credit will be approved.

*Remember!* Every credit grantor has its own form of processing.

## Establishing Credit for the First Time

Everyone needs to start somewhere when establishing credit. I hear from people who want to establish credit but are turned down because they never have had credit. This section explains five different methods for establishing credit if you have never had it before.

### Five Methods for Establishing Credit

**1. Open a personal secured loan.** With a personal secured loan, you can open up a savings or CD account from which you draw interest. The amount of your deposit depends on the bank's minimum deposit requirements and what you can afford. If there are no minimum deposit requirements, make a $300 to $2,000 deposit. Once you have deposited the money, ask the bank for a loan against it. In exchange, you are securing the loan with the money in your savings or CD account. The bank avoids the risk of your not repaying the loan because it can take the money out of your account. During the time of the loan, you don't have access to your account and thus can't draw money out of it.

Each bank has its own requirements, but most will not lend you 100 percent of your deposit, maybe only 80 to 90 percent. Many banks will allow you one to three years to repay the loan. Payments on the loan will be arranged by the bank; some, for example, don't require any payment until the end of the loan period.

Remember that you are trying to build a good credit rating. By making payments on a regular basis, you will begin to establish a good payment pattern that will be reported to the credit bureaus. Repeat this process with other banks so that you'll have more than one "good" account reported, showing your reliability and likelihood of repaying debts.

**2. Merchants.** Merchants are another source for establishing credit: jewelry, furniture, tire, and appliance stores usually offer credit. Before actually applying, tell several stores that you have never had credit but would like to establish it with them. Select an item you would like to purchase and find out if the store selling it will allow you to set up a 90-day account. If the store agrees, be sure you make the required payment before the due date and that the store reports a good payment pattern to its credit reporting agency or agencies. Find out before you get the credit if the particular merchant subscribes and reports to a major reporting agency and the name of the agency.

Repeat this procedure at least two times before applying for a major credit card.

**3. Secured credit cards.** This is another sure way to establish credit. A secured card is one that is given to a consumer and secured with a deposit at a bank that offers this type of program. (Secured cards are discussed further in Chapter 2.) Banks that offer a secured program are hard to find. You can call your local banks and savings and loans or check your newspaper for the institutions offering this program.

**4. Cosigner.** If you do not want to get a secured credit card to establish or reestablish your credit, you can ask a friend or relative to cosign on a loan or credit card. What's good for you, however, could be risky for the cosigner. A person who completes an application for credit with you is responsible for the debt if you fail to pay back the money. A cosigner must qualify for the line of credit and sign papers accepting responsibility for the payment if you default.

The account that is opened for you with a cosigner, who has guaranteed the loan, is usually reported to the credit reporting bureaus in both names if it is a guaranteed loan. If you don't make the payments, it will be reported on your credit report as well as on the cosigner's report. If the payments are made when due, on the other hand, your rating will be good—a big advantage when establishing a good payment pattern.

**5. A friend or relative.** A friend or relative can help you establish credit by requesting a credit card in your name from a credit card company with whom the friend or relative has established credit. Once a credit card is issued to the person responsible for payment, a card issuer often grants that person's request for an additional card in another person's name.

The best way to approach this type of situation is to tell the friend or relative to keep the card (as you'll not be using it) but to request the credit grantor to report the payment pattern on your credit report. That way a positive credit rating will be established. Your goal is not to use the credit card, only to establish a good payment pattern. Once you've established your own credit history, the friend or relative can cancel your card, which has no effect on your credit report.

Before applying for any major credit cards or department store cards, make sure that you have built up a good payment record. Apply for a department store card first. Wait three to six months before you apply for a Visa or MasterCard card, being sure your credit report shows a positive payment pattern.

Once you have been approved for credit cards, *do not over-extend your credit.* Use only one or two credit cards so you will not lose control of your finances. Any other cards that you have should be put in a safe deposit box in case of an emergency. The danger of too many cards is that you will overextend yourself and fall behind in repaying the balances. Balances shown at the end of your statement should be paid off as soon as possible, preferably when the statement becomes due.

Fill out the Establishing Credit Worksheet.

## Credit and the Senior Citizen

Securing credit is as important for older/retired people as it is for younger people. Without proper knowledge and education about the credit system, many older people are turned down for credit. Older women appear to have more problems than men, stemming from the fact that many have had (or still have) only an authorization to use a credit card issued in their husband's name and are not themselves responsible for any payments. Thus, these women have no credit history reported in their own name.

If you have always paid cash for your purchases, you too may find it difficult to open a new line of credit because the report on you states "no credit history." If you are living on a reduced salary or pension, it also may be more difficult to obtain a line of credit because you are considered to have "insufficient income."

Under the federal Equal Credit Opportunity Act (ECOA), a creditor cannot deny you credit or terminate any existing credit because of your age.

## Establishing Credit Worksheet

If you need to establish or reestablish credit, answer the following questions. List five banks where you could set up a savings account.

_____

_____

_____

_____

_____

Contact four merchants to see if they have first-time buyer applications for establishing credit. List the names of the merchants.

_____

_____

_____

_____

_____

Write for credit applications from two banks that offer secured credit cards. List the banks and their addresses.

_____

_____

_____

_____

_____

List three friends and relatives who might act as cosigners for you on a loan and/or might request an additional credit card in your name.

_____

_____

_____

_____

_____

## Creditors' Evaluation

When you apply for credit, one major criterion for credit approval, as I've mentioned before, is your ability to repay the debt, and ability is evaluated by your current income. It may be of concern to a credit grantor if you are retired or employed part-time. Creditors must consider the types of income an older person receives—for example, a current salary, Social Security, pension(s), and other retirement benefits.

When applying for credit, you should let the creditor know about your assets or sources of income, such as real estate, savings and checking accounts, money market funds, certificates of deposit, and stocks and bonds.

Because creditors check your credit history, you should know what your credit report says about you before making any application for credit. Make sure all your accounts are listed and are being accurately reported. The same evaluation is done for qualification for a line of credit. *Income* and *credit history* are the two primary considerations.

Under the Equal Credit Opportunity Act, a creditor cannot automatically close or change the terms of a joint account solely because of the death of your spouse. (A joint account is one for which both spouses applied and signed the credit agreement.) The creditor may, however, ask you to update your credit application or reapply, particularly if the initial acceptance was based on all or part of your spouse's income and the creditor suspects your income is inadequate to support the line of credit.

Once a reapplication is submitted, the creditor will determine whether to continue to extend you credit or make changes on your credit limit. The creditor must respond in writing to your application within 30 days. While the application is being processed, you may use your line of credit with no interruptions. If, for some reason, your application is turned down, you must be informed of the reason. Sometimes an application is turned down if the initial acceptance was based on all or part of your spouse's income and your income now seems inadequate.

To ensure protection should a spouse die, it is important to know what kinds of credit accounts you have; there are three different kinds.

## *Kinds of Accounts*

1. An *individual account* is one opened in one person's name. The acceptance of a credit application is based only on that person's income and assets.

2. A *joint account* is one opened in the name of two people, usually a husband and wife. Acceptance of the credit application is based on the income of either person or both. Both people are liable for any debts because both have signed the credit application.

3. A *user account* is one in which the names of more than one person may appear on an account or charge card that is based on the income and assets of just one of those people. That person is the one who is legally responsible for any debts.

**In the event of death or discrimination.** A joint account is the only type of account that provides protection against the account's being closed because of a death.

It is always a good idea to have credit not only jointly, if you are married, but also individually to protect you from any account closures.

If you think you have been discriminated against in any way by a creditor who has denied you credit, you may write to the federal agency named in the letter denying you credit. (Any letter turning down your request for credit will have the name and address of the appropriate federal agency.) If you do write, it is important that you remember and report all the facts. Make sure you have written down any oral statements or discussions that took place with the creditor. Keep copies of all letters or correspondence, and submit them with your letter to the agency.

## Women and Credit

Donna had been using her husband's charge cards for several years; when the bills came due, she would pay them promptly. Donna decided to apply for a credit card in her own name and was rejected because no record was found when the creditor ran a credit report on her. The information about her husband's open charge accounts was not on Donna's credit report.

## Account Status Worksheet

List all your credit accounts and identify each as individual, joint, or user.

| Creditor | Individual | Joint | User |
|---|---|---|---|
|  |  |  |  |
|  |  |  |  |
|  |  |  |  |
|  |  |  |  |
|  |  |  |  |
|  |  |  |  |
|  |  |  |  |
|  |  |  |  |
|  |  |  |  |
|  |  |  |  |
|  |  |  |  |
|  |  |  |  |
|  |  |  |  |
|  |  |  |  |
|  |  |  |  |
|  |  |  |  |
|  |  |  |  |
|  |  |  |  |
|  |  |  |  |

Kathy was recently divorced and took back her maiden name. She had several good credit accounts in her married name, but when she applied for new credit with her maiden name, no record of her credit history was found.

Jane was 25 years old and a single woman who paid cash for all her purchases. She had never established credit in her name and didn't know where to begin to get credit because she had no prior credit history.

These situations could have been avoided if these women had planned ahead on how to establish their own credit history.

## Establishing Credit

Now more than ever women are in the workforce and need to establish credit in their own name. Many married women feel they need to use their husband's credit cards and don't worry about having their own. Whether married or single, it is important to have credit in your own name. You never know when you may need it for an emergency. If something happens to your spouse, you don't know if you will be able to reestablish yourself in the credit world. It is especially important to have credit in your name if the accounts were in your spouse's name. Even though you were a user of the account and paid the bills, you still would not have a credit record.

The Equal Credit Opportunity Act was designed to prevent discrimination against women in the world of credit. You may not be denied credit just because you are a woman or on the basis of your status as married, single, widowed, divorced, or separated.

A good place to start when trying to see what payment history has been reported on you is to order a credit report from all three major credit reporting bureaus—Experian, Trans Union, and Equifax. Each agency may be reporting different information. Be sure to examine the report carefully.

If no payment record is found, you need to take action. If the creditors you have made payments to in the past have failed to report the accounts on your credit file and a statement on the report indicates "no record is found," you'll be denied credit.

When a women is widowed, divorced, or wants credit in her own name, a credit application can be turned down because all her previous accounts were in her husband's name. A single woman may have problems after she marries because the accounts held in her maiden name may not have been transferred to a file with her married name.

## Building a Good Credit Report

Here are four guidelines to start building a good credit report.

1. If you have had credit before under your maiden name, contact the creditor and give your new married name and pertinent information. Ask the creditor to update their files and enter it on your credit report under your married name.

2. If you have shared accounts with your husband or former husband, make sure these creditors are reporting the accounts on your credit report. If they aren't, ask them to do so and to update your report.

3. If you are married, notify each creditor that you want accounts you share with your husband reported on both credit reports.

4. If you were married or divorced recently and changed your name, ask your creditors to change your name on their accounts. Once these accounts are in your new name, your credit history should be updated.

## Protecting Yourself

Once you have established your own credit report, it will be easier for you to establish new credit in your name. That is an excellent safeguard in case of any future emergency.

Because every woman needs to know how she can be protected, the following list offers four suggestions:

1. When applying for credit, you do not have to use Miss, Mrs., or Ms. with your name.

2. Creditors cannot ask questions about birth control or your desire to have children. They cannot assume that by having children your income will drop.

3. Creditors must consider all employment income, whether from full-time or part-time employment, as reported on your application. Child support and alimony payments must also be considered as income.

4. Creditors cannot refuse to open a credit account because of your sex or marital status. You can choose to use your married name or maiden name, and if you are creditworthy, your husband does not need to cosign your account.

   Creditors may not ask for information about your husband unless your income is not high enough, unless your account is going to be used by your husband and he is paying your debts, or unless you live in a community property state (Arizona, California, Idaho, Louisiana, Nevada, New Mexico, Texas, and Washington).

If you feel you have been discriminated against because of your sex, you can file a complaint with the Federal Trade Commission.

## Sample Letter to Request Dual Reporting

ABC Company
Credit Division
1111 Sixth St.
Anytown, NY 00123

(Date)

Dear Sir or Madam:

Under the Equal Credit Opportunity Act, I am requesting that you report all credit information on this account in both names.

Account number: _____

Names on account: _____

_____

Address: _____

City, state, zip: _____

Signature (either spouse) _____

## Credit Denials

Being approved for credit may not be as easy as it sounds. Several factors can pose obstacles to your being approved for certain kinds of credit—in other words, credit denial.

### Factors That Can Lead to a Denial of Credit

**No credit history.** Someone who has never had an installment type loan that would appear on a credit report has no credit history. When a credit report is run on an individual and no payment pattern or history is found, the credit report will come back with a statement "No Record Found." This is almost as detrimental as having bad credit because a credit grantor cannot distinguish a payment pattern and will usually deny the application.

**Negative or derogatory credit.**  A credit report contains codes that rate a person according to the items on the report and indicates positive or negative information. The negative items that show up can be charge-offs, late payments, a delinquent account, repossessions, judgments, tax liens, and similar factors.

**Inquiries.**  Any time you apply for credit, the creditor—XYZ Company for example—will run a credit report. It is then reported on any subsequent reports that an inquiry was made on a particular date by XYZ Company. If you were turned down for the credit, the next creditor will more than likely turn you down too. Excessive inquiries within a six-month period will hurt your chances of getting credit. Five inquiries with denials will probably cause the application to be rejected.

If it is you that requests a copy of your credit report directly from a credit reporting agency, no inquiry will appear.

**Overextended.**  When creditors evaluate your application, they take into consideration your monthly income and your monthly expenses. If you are already too far extended or in debt, they will deny your application. (Refer back to the Debt to Ratio Worksheet.)

**Self-employed.**  Creditors feel people who are self-employed pose a greater risk than do those who are employed by others. A person must be self-employed for approximately two years when applying for a mortgage or other credit to be considered. Each creditor has its own guidelines, so be sure to find out what these guidelines are before filling out a credit application.

**Public notices.**  Public notices are warnings in essence that have been recorded with a county official and are available for anyone to see. Examples of public notices include bankruptcies, judgments, tax liens, notices of default, and foreclosures.

The following is a list of many reasons an applicant may be denied credit by a bank:

- Insufficient income
- Too short a period of employment
- Sufficient credit obligations
- Failure to pay previous obligations as agreed
- Garnishment, attachment, judgment, foreclosure, repossession

- Bankruptcy (under Chapters 7, 11, or 13)
- Insufficient income for the amount requested
- No previous bank borrowing experience within the past 18 months (excluding a mortgage)
- Inability to verify income
- Inability to verify employment
- Incomplete credit application
- Terms and conditions requested by applicant unacceptable
- Present bank references established less than six months before
- Foreigners without permanent resident status (no green card)
- P.O. box given as mailing address
- Unlisted telephone number
- No checking or savings account

Any time there is a denial of credit, the creditor must notify the applicant in writing. The denial letter must include the reason for the denial and indicate which credit bureau was used in reaching the decision. You may request a credit report free from the agency listed provided the request is made within 60 days from the date of the denial letter (see the Sample Letter of Denial).

## Credit Reporting Agencies

There are three major credit reporting agencies in the United States: Experian, Trans Union, and Equifax. Each of them has credit information on as many as 170 million Americans. The credit reporting agencies store information in their computers on every individual who has a credit record. The subscribers are the creditors who report information to the reporting agencies. Information is reported on the consumers' accounts by the creditors. The creditors are the main source to report on an individual's payment history. The different sources could be a department store, a bank, a car dealer, or sometimes public records, for example, tax liens, judgments, and bankruptcies. Creditors report to credit reporting agencies monthly about consumers' payment habits, but they report only to agencies to which they subscribe (i.e., are paying members). That is why an individual may have a certain item on one credit report but not on another. Both positive and negative accounts appear on credit reports.

## Sample Letter of Credit Denial

May 21, 1996

ABC Bank
1111 Main
Anytown, MD 33333

Michael Smith
2233 Flower St.
Anytown, CA 11111

Dear Mr. Smith,

Your application for a Visa charge card has been denied. The reasons are as follows:

<u>Insufficient income and failure to pay previous obligations as agreed</u>

The information obtained in a consumer report was from Experian, P.O. Box 2104, Allen, TX 75013.

When credit is denied because of credit information contained in a consumer report, you have the right to inspect and receive a copy of that report. You may do so by contacting the consumer reporting agency that is listed.

The following paragraph contains important information concerning your rights.

Equal Credit Opportunity Act
Notice

The federal Equal Credit Opportunity Act (15 U.S.C. § 1691) prohibits creditors from discriminating against credit applicants and/or existing customers on the basis of race, color, religion, national origin, sex, marital status, or age (provided that the applicant has the capacity to enter into a binding contract); because all or part of the applicant's income derives from any public assistance program; or because the applicant has in good faith exercised any right under the Consumer Credit Protection Act.

# Credit Denial Worksheet

List the institutions to which you applied for credit and their responses.

| Institution | Date Letter Received | Reason for Denial | Reporting Agency | Date Report Requested |
|---|---|---|---|---|
| | | | | |
| | | | | |
| | | | | |
| | | | | |
| | | | | |
| | | | | |
| | | | | |
| | | | | |
| | | | | |
| | | | | |
| | | | | |
| | | | | |
| | | | | |
| | | | | |
| | | | | |
| | | | | |
| | | | | |
| | | | | |
| | | | | |
| | | | | |
| | | | | |
| | | | | |
| | | | | |
| | | | | |
| | | | | |
| | | | | |
| | | | | |
| | | | | |
| | | | | |

## Limits on Negative Information

There is a limit on how long certain items may remain on the files of credit reporting agencies. Reports of bankruptcies must be removed after ten years. Reports of judgments, tax liens, and most other unfavorable information, such as slow payments, charge-offs, repossessions, delinquent accounts, and the like, must be removed after seven years.

Do not confuse your local credit bureaus with major credit reporting agencies. Your local credit bureaus have access to the major reporting agencies, such as Experian, Trans Union, and Equifax, and many times will combine the agencies' information into one report. This is often done when you apply for a home loan and more than one credit report is required. This is done because sometimes the three agencies carry different accounts and information.

## Authorization

An application you submit for credit usually has a paragraph that states in these or similar words: "By signing below, I authorize XYZ Company to check my credit history and exchange information about how I handle my account with proper persons and with credit bureaus if I am issued credit." By signing this type of statement, you are authorizing a credit check and authorizing the creditor to report your account to its credit reporting agency or agencies.

## Don't Give Out Information

No one may have credit information from your credit file without direct permission from you. Be selective about those you authorize to check your credit report.

Nancy came to the office one day for assistance with her credit report because of excessive inquiries listed on the report during a three-day period. When questioned about the inquiries, she indicated that she had spoken to someone on the telephone about a car purchase and had given the person her name, address, and Social Security number. Without her knowledge the car company contacted several banks to try to qualify her for a loan. The four banks contacted made credit check inquiries, which were conducted without her permission but were reflected on her credit report. Because the company that authorized the credit investigation did not have permission to contact the banks, Nancy got in touch with the car company and told the company she had never given authorization to make these credit inquiries. No authorization was in writing, and she gave the company two weeks to remove the inquiries from her credit report. This was done promptly by the agencies involved. The moral of the story is that it is important to know your legal rights to avoid similar mishaps.

## Get Your Own Credit Report

When applying for a car, home loan, or store credit, have in hand an updated credit report on yourself and show it to the potential creditor. Don't let a potential creditor run a credit report on you unless the creditor indicates your application will be approved: this will eliminate having an inquiry on your report. And as we've seen, an inquiry can work against you if you don't qualify for the credit. Remember, five inquiries with rejections will make it more difficult to get an approval on most credit applications.

## Credit Denied

When you've applied for credit and your application has been turned down, the creditor must send you a letter within 60 days stating the reason you were denied the credit. The letter should include the name and address of the credit reporting agency that issued the report on your file. Whenever an application is turned down, you are entitled to a free credit report from the credit reporting agency listed in the denial letter. You must request a copy of the credit report within 60 days of the denial letter and should include a copy of the denial letter with your request. If the denial letter is not available, state in your letter to the credit reporting agency the name of the company that refused you credit (see Sample Credit Report Request Form: B).

**Get a free credit report.** You are entitled to a free credit report if you have been turned down for credit, employment, insurance, or a rental dwelling because of information in your credit report within the preceding 60 days.

## Have Your Own Report

It is a good idea to have an updated credit report on yourself from all the major credit reporting agencies that report in your community: Experian, Trans Union, or Equifax. If you are not sure which agencies are dominant in your community, call a local bank or mortgage company to see which agency or agencies it gets its credit reports from. Each city and state is different. If you have not been turned down for credit, the credit reporting agency will charge a fee for the report. Every state sets its own fee that you can find out by calling Experian, Trans Union, and Equifax directly. Each credit bureau has an 800 telephone number that you can find through directory assistance.

When requesting a copy of your credit report, remember that a husband and wife will not have combined reports. Each has an individual report, which applies even if the account is a joint account. You must send fees for each report; for example, send $8 for the husband and $8 for the wife.

## Ordering Your Credit Report

To request a copy of your credit report, include the following information:

- Full name, including middle initial and generation, such as Jr., Sr., II, or III
- Address with zip code
- Previous address with zip code if you have moved within the past five years
- Social Security number
- Date of birth
- Spouse's name
- For verification a photocopy of a billing statement, driver's license, or other documents that link your name with the requested report and the address to which it is to be mailed (Some bureaus require two forms of identification.)

## Checking for Inaccuracies

When you receive a copy of your report, there will be instructions showing you how to read each account and how you are being rated. Make sure the items are being accurately reported. Many times there is inaccurate information on your report that must be corrected before you can apply for credit. Credit repair will be covered in later chapters.

Because understanding your credit report can be difficult, you may write or call Professional Credit Counselors, 1100 Irvine Blvd., #541, Tustin, CA 92780 (714-541-2637), to get a personalized credit analysis of your credit report.

Credit bureaus are regulated by the Federal Trade Commission under the provisions of the Fair Credit Reporting Act and the Consumer Credit Reporting Reform Act of 1996. To receive a copy of the law, write to the Federal Trade Commission, 6th & Pennsylvania Ave., N.W., Washington, DC 20580.

You may request copies of your credit report from the three major credit reporting agencies or refer to your telephone directory for the phone numbers and addresses of those with offices in your area. If you are unable to locate one near you to get your credit report, write the national headquarters listed below:

Experian
P.O. Box 2104
Allen, TX 75013

Trans Union
P.O. Box 390
Springfield, PA 19064

Equifax
P.O. Box 740193
Atlanta, GA 30374-0193

## Credit Bureaus Worksheet

List the names and addresses of the major credit bureaus in your area.

| Name | Address | Date Requested |
|------|---------|----------------|
|      |         |                |
|      |         |                |
|      |         |                |
|      |         |                |
|      |         |                |
|      |         |                |
|      |         |                |
|      |         |                |
|      |         |                |
|      |         |                |
|      |         |                |
|      |         |                |
|      |         |                |
|      |         |                |

## Obtaining and Evaluating Credit Records

The first step in evaluating your credit report is to obtain a copy from the three major credit reporting agencies (Experian, Trans Union, and Equifax) by following the instructions in the preceding section.

Once you receive a copy of your credit report, determine the status of your credit file. You should attempt to remove all inaccurate, incorrect, incomplete, and erroneous information. An explanation page will help you analyze the report.

On the Experian report, the most important thing to look for is the asterisk (*) located on the far left side next to the entry. The asterisk indicates a derogatory or negative entry. Read what the entry says; for example, late payments, collection accounts, charge-offs, or a public notice

## Sample Credit Report Request Form: A

Experian
P.O. Box 2104
Allen, TX 75013

Please send me a copy of my current credit report. I am enclosing the required $8 fee.

Name:
Address:
City, state, zip:
Previous address (past five years):
Social Security number:
Year of birth:

Thank you,

(Sign your name)

(Use this format if you have not been turned down for credit recently. Enclose a copy of your drivers license or utility bill showing your name and address; this is for identification purposes.)

such as a bankruptcy, tax lien, or judgment. Study everything on the report carefully to see if inaccurate information is being reported.

Analyze if the statements are 100 percent correct and accurate. For example, an item that is listed paid was 90 days late: 5/95 (date and year). You may have been late, but not 90 days late. You may not have ever been late but that is what is being reported and is an item that you should dispute.

Equifax reports are formatted differently than those of Experian and Trans Union. Equifax's ratings are as follows: *R* (means revolving account) and *I* (means installment account). In an installment credit agreement, a consumer signs a contract to repay a fixed amount of credit in equal payments over a specified period of time. Automobiles, furni-

## Sample Credit Report Request Form: B

Trans Union
P.O. Box 390
Springfield, PA 19064

Please send me a copy of my current credit report. I have been recently turned down for credit by _____ .

Name:
Address:
City, state, zip:
Previous address (past five years):
Social Security number:
Year of birth:

Thank you,

(Sign your name)

(Use this format if you have been turned down for credit within the past 60 days. Enclose a copy of your drivers license or utility bill showing your name and address; this is for identification purposes.)

ture, and major appliances are often purchased on an installment basis; and personal loans too are usually repaid in installments.

In a revolving credit agreement, a consumer has the option of paying in full each month or making a minimum payment based on the amount of the outstanding balance. Department stores, gas and oil companies, and banks typically issue credit cards based on a revolving credit plan.

In an open 30-day agreement, a consumer promises to repay the full balance owed each month. Travel and entertainment charge cards and charge accounts with local businesses often require repayment on this basis.

Under the status section located on the right-hand portion of the Equifax report are ratings that may say *I-3* (meaning you were three months late on payments) or *R-9* (meaning the company placed the account in collection or charged it off). The Equifax report shows the ratings under the column marked CS. Anything other than an *R-1* or *I-1* rating is negative.

A Trans Union report must be read differently from those of Experian and Equifax. The Trans Union credit report has the negative and derogatory information listed with brackets (> <) on the upper portion of the report. The lower portion of the report indicates the accounts that carry no adverse information.

## Rating Descriptions

The following descriptions are used to indicate payment history on credit reports:

Bk Adj Plan—Debit included in or completed through a Chapter 13 bankruptcy

Bk Liq Reo—Debit included in or discharged through a Chapter 7 or 11 bankruptcy

Charge-off—Unpaid balance reported as a loss by the credit grantor, who writes you off

Clos INAC—Closed inactive account

CLOS NP AA—Credit line closed/not paying as agreed

Coll Acct—Account seriously past due/account assigned to attorney, collection agency, or credit grantor's internal collection department

CR CD Lost—Credit card lost or stolen

CR Ln Clos—Credit line closed for reason unknown or by consumer request/may be an unpaid balance

CR Ln Rnst—Account now available for use and in good standing.

Curr Acct—Either an open or closed account in good standing

Cur was Col—Current account was a collection account

Cur was Dl—Current account was past due

Cur was For—Foreclosure was started on current account

Cur was 30-2 or 3, 4, 5, 6—Current account was 30 days past due two, three, four, five, six times

Cur was 60, or 90, 120, 150, 180—Current account was 60, or 90, 120, 150, 180 days late on payment

Deceased—Consumer deceased

Delinq 60, or 90, 120, 150, 180—Account 60, or 90, 120, 150, 180 days late

Del was 90—Account was delinquent 90 days/now 30 or 60 days late

Gov Claim—Claim filed with government for insured portion or balance on an educational loan

Foreclosure—Credit grantor sold collateral to settle a mortgage that is in default

Inquiry—A copy of the credit report sent to the credit grantor that has just requested it

Ins Claim—Claim filed for payment of insured portion of balance

Judgment—Lawsuit resulted in a judgment against you but not paid

Lien—Federal, state, or county taxes owed

Not Pd AA—Account not being paid as agreed

Paid Acct—Closed account with a zero balance and not rated by credit grantor

Paid Status—Closed account, paid satisfactorily

Pd by Dler—Credit grantor paid by company that originally sold the merchandise

Pd Chg-off—Paid account that was a charge-off

Pd Coll Acc—Paid account that was a collection account

Paid not AA—Paid account but some payments made past agreed due dates

Pd Repo—Paid account that was a repossession

Pd was 30—Paid account that was past due 30 days

Pd was 30-2 or 4,5,6+—Paid account that was past due 30 days, 2, 3, 4, 5, 6, or more times

Pd was 60, or 90, 120, 150, 180—Paid account that was late 60, or 90, 120, 150, 180 days

Redmd Repo—Account was a repossession, now redeemed

Refinanced—Account was renewed or refinanced

Repo—Merchandise taken back by credit grantor and outstanding balance may remain

SCNL—Credit grantor cannot locate consumer

Settled—Account legally paid in full for less than the full balance

Volun Repo—Voluntary repossession

30 Day Del—Account past due 30 days

30-2, 3, 4, 5, 6+ times—Account past due 30 days 2, 3, 4, 5, 6, or more times

30 was 60—Account was delinquent 60 days and now 30 days late

## Additional Ratings–Manner of Payment

In some reports an *I* or *R* will precede the following entries:

00—Too new to rate; approved but not used or rated

01—Pays within 30 days of billing; pays account as agreed

02—Pays in more than 30 days but not more than 60 days, or not more than one payment due

03—Pays in more than 60 days but not more than 90 days, or not more than two payments due

04—Pays in more than 90 days but not more than 120 days, or not more than three or more payments due

05—Pays in 120 days or more

07—Making regular payments under wage-earner plan or similar arrangement

08—Repossession

8A—Voluntary repossession

8R—Legal repossession

09—Bad debt; placed for collection, suit, judgment, charge-off, bankruptcy: skip

9B—Collection account

UR—Unrated

It is important to remember that, if you are married, you and your spouse must apply separately for your credit reports even if you have obtained your credit jointly. Include fees to cover both reports.

As mentioned before, you can write or call Professional Credit Counselors, 1100 Irvine Blvd., #541, Tustin, CA 92780 (714·541·2637), to get a personalized credit analysis of your credit report.

## The Dispute Process

If you have found errors in your credit report, write to the credit bureau to dispute the entries you feel are inaccurately reported. Study each entry to see if the item indicates the correct status. Are the dates correct? The amounts correct? Account numbers correct? Study each entry carefully. If any are inaccurate, you may file a dispute. Send the dispute by regular mail and you can expect an updated report in 45 to 60 days from the date you mailed it. The corrections and deletions should be reflected on the updated report.

When a dispute is filed with a credit bureau, it is the creditor's responsibility to respond to the credit bureau's inquiry about the disputed item. The credit reporting agency will complete its investigation with the creditor within 30 days of receiving your dispute. If the dispute is not answered by the creditor or it is unverifiable, the item in dispute must be removed from the files of the credit reporting agencies.

If you are not satisfied with the results, you may add a 100-word statement to the credit report indicating your side of the story.

## Fair Credit Reporting Act

Being familiar with the Fair Credit Reporting Act and the Consumer Credit Reporting Reform Act of 1996 will help you when you begin disputing any inaccurate information on your credit report. (You can request a free copy of the Fair Credit Reporting Act from the Federal Trade Commission.)

### Important Provisions

The law was designed to provide guidelines on what a credit reporting agency can or cannot do to you. Some key purposes of the act are to protect your privacy and assure accurate reporting and proper utilization of reported credit information.

There are two main areas you need to be knowledgeable about when trying to rid your credit report of inaccurate information. The Fair Credit Reporting Act gives you the right to see what your credit report says about you. You, however, must initiate the report as a credit reporting bureau cannot run a credit report on you without your *written* authorization, and the bureau may charge a fee for the report.

Information on your credit report that is not complete or accurate can be disputed with the credit bureau unless the bureau feels the dispute is frivolous or irrelevant. If, after an investigation, the item you are disputing is found to be inaccurate or can no longer be verified, the item must be removed. If you're not satisfied with the results of your dispute, you can write a 100-word statement on each of the items you feel are inaccurate.

# **C**hapter 4

# **Why So Many Questions?**
## Applying for Credit

### Making Your Credit Application

As you can see before applying for credit, you must do your homework. You need to determine the type of credit that will fit your needs. For example, if you want to take a family vacation, a bank may reject your application because it sees a trip as a poor reason for borrowing money. It may be better for you to use your credit cards for the vacation, getting a cash advance or using the card for reservations and purchases. Because credit cards usually have a grace period before payment is due, you'd have use of the money without interest. Try to pay the card off before the due date to avoid future interest charges.

Whenever you're applying for a credit card or any other type of credit, you should be aware of what your credit reports say about you. Before sending in your application, call the creditor's processing department to find out which reporting agency is used. If it is Equifax, and you know your Equifax credit report looks good, then submit your application. If the credit grantor informs you it uses Trans Union, and you know that your Trans Union report is showing negative, but inaccurate, information, do not submit the application. Request the credit grantor to check your Equifax report only. If the answer is "yes," put a note on the application that you are only authorizing a credit check with Equifax for your complete credit file. If the credit grantor does not indicate it will honor your request, do not submit an application. It will only result in an inquiry and a rejection of the application. Go back instead and work on correcting the negative inaccurate entry on your credit report(s) before applying for credit. Generally, one negative item won't hurt you as long as there is enough positive credit on the report to offset the negative.

To avoid having inquiries appear on your credit report when applying for a car or home, or any type of merchant credit, have an updated credit report on hand. The creditor or bank can evaluate the report immediately without running another one and thus avoid an inquiry that will show on your credit file. If the creditor indicates that the application will be approved, then go ahead and authorize a credit report.

**NEVER give your name, address, or Social Security number** to anyone over the telephone when you are applying for credit. It will only cause another inquiry to be added to your credit report.

When filling out a credit application, be sure to put on it the items you know are on your credit report. Credit grantors receive so many applications that often they don't verify your income. Make sure, however, that in case a grantor does call to verify your income with your employer, the income you've stated on the application is correct.

## Track Your Application

Apply for credit cards with aggressive banks. These banks distribute applications all over town. Many out-of-state banks are anxious for your business; nationwide banks can approve Visa or MasterCard applications in any state. (See the list of nationwide banks in chapter 3.) Most banks are restricted to servicing accounts in their state only.

Once you have applied for a Visa and MasterCard, keep records of the results. (See sample and actual Tracking Credit Applications Worksheet.) Not every institution will approve your application, and it is important to know the reasons for any credit denials. Keeping track of your applications and results will help you in reapplying. When you are declined credit, the institution that denied your application must send you a letter indicating the reason and which credit reporting agency was used to gather information for your file. Be sure to send for a copy of the credit report within 60 days of a denial so you can get it free.

## Screen the Banks

Do not approach just any bank or savings and loan association (S&L) when applying for credit cards. Before applying, screen the banks. There are usually major differences in interest rates, loan fees, payment requirements, and so on. The following is a list of questions to ask:

**Which credit reporting agency do you use—Experian, Equifax, or Trans Union?** If the bank responds that it uses Experian and you know your Trans Union credit report looks better, ask if the bank would use Trans Union instead of Experian and write across the application, "PLEASE USE TRANS UNION TO GET MY COMPLETE CREDIT FILE."

**What is your annual yearly fee?** Most banks and S&Ls charge a yearly fee that can range from $18 to $40. Occasionally, you may find a few institutions that charge no annual fee.

**What is your interest rate and how is it calculated?** Institutions that grant loans and issue credit cards charge an annual percentage rate (APR) for the use of their money. To figure the total cost of a loan in dollars, multiply the monthly payments by the total number of months of the loan. Then subtract the total amount borrowed from the total monthly payments and you'll see how much you're paying in interest for the use of the bank's money. For credit cards, some banks calculate interest on a daily basis. That means once a purchase or charge is made, the interest charges begin to accumulate. Other banks calculate interest on a pro-rated interest, which means no interest is charged until the billing cycle.

In your monthly statement is a section that will tell you how much your finance or interest charge is for that month. When you subtract the finance or interest charge from your payment for that month, the difference is the principal that is deducted from the balance.

**What cards do you issue, and what are the limits?** Some banks will offer Visa cards only or MasterCard cards only, and some will offer both. When applying for a card from a bank that offers both Visa and MasterCard cards, check the box on the application for both cards. Find out what the maximum limit is on the card; for example, one bank's maximum credit limit may be $2,000. Some institutions offer a premium card with a credit limit from $5,000 to $50,000. If you feel you can qualify for a high credit limit, get an application for the premium cards when requesting the applications.

**How often does your bank review increases in credit card limits?**
Some banks review increases on request or every three or four months. To get an increase, be sure to pay your statement before the due date. If you can't pay the total balance, pay four times your monthly payment; for example, if your monthly payment is $25, pay $100 if it fits into your budget. Do not go over your credit limit, as it only works against you.

**What do you charge for a cash advance? What is the maximum cash advance I can withdraw?** Some banks charge a percentage of your cash advance or a flat fee. Many banks allow you the full credit limit for an advance cash withdrawal; for example, a $2,000 credit limit equals a $2,000 cash advance. Some banks may restrict the amount of the cash advance. It is important to know all the options.

**Do I have to have a bank account with your bank to get a Visa or MasterCard credit card?** Many times it is necessary to have an account with the bank before they'll issue a Visa or MasterCard card.

These questions should be answered to your satisfaction before you apply to any banking institution. Use your best judgment in determining the right institution for you.

Always have a master application form completed for reference. You can use the information from the master application in completing other applications. By using the master application form, you'll be consistent with your entries on applications submitted to the companies or institutions with whom you are applying for credit.

## Read Everything

When filling out your application, be sure it is legible. Neatness is a must, so print or type the information. Many applications are rejected because the lender can't read them.

Attach anything that you feel may improve your chances of approval: income tax forms or, if you are self-employed, 1099 forms.

Never make false or misleading entries on your loan application. Always be truthful.

## Questions for Lenders

Bank or other institution's name _____ Date _____

1. Which credit reporting agency do you use—Experian, Equifax, or Trans Union?

2. What is your annual yearly fee?

3. What is your interest rate and how is it calculated?

4. What cards do you issue, and what are the limits issued?

5. How often does your bank review increases in credit card limits?

6. What do you charge for a cash advance? What is the maximum cash advance I can withdraw?

7. Do I have to have a bank account with your bank to get a Visa or Master-Card credit card?

Every application you complete for credit cards has disclosures. Under the Truth in Lending Act, all lending institutions are required to disclose to the consumer the following:

- The monthly finance charge, which includes interest charges and service fees
- The APR (i.e., the monthly finance charge multiplied by 12)
- Type of interest rate—fixed or variable and, if variable, how it is calculated
- The range of balances to which the interest rate applies, if there is more than one rate (Frequently with a cash advance, the interest rate will be different.)
- The number of days you have to pay off the balance with no interest charged
- How the balance on which the interest is imposed is calculated
- Any annual, periodic, or membership fee
- The amount charged for a late payment, over-the-limit fee, or cash advance fee

## Sample Tracking for Credit Applications Worksheet

| Creditor's Name & Address | Date Application Mailed | Approved Date | Declined: Date & Reason |
|---|---|---|---|
| XYZ Company 2218 Main Anytown, NM 77111 | 3/5/96 | 4/10/96 | |
| UPP Company 1132 Jeffrey Anytown, AL 33244 | | | 4/15/96 Slow payments |

## Authorizing the Lender

At the bottom of an application is an authorization form that may, for example, state the following:

> By signing below I authorize XYZ Company to check my credit history and exchange information about how I handle my account with proper persons, affiliates, and credit bureaus if I am issued a card. I authorize my employer, my bank, and any other references listed above to release and/or verify information to XYZ Company and its affiliates in order to determine my eligibility for the XYZ credit card and any future extension of credit. If I ask, I will be told whether consumer reports on me were requested and the names of the credit bureaus, with their addresses, that provided the reports. I certify that the information provided is accurate. I have read and understand the credit terms.

By signing this authorization, you are giving the lender permission to review your credit report. Once you are approved for credit, the creditor can report your payment pattern to the credit bureaus. You are also stating that the information in the application is accurate; if not, the lender can reject the application. At a later time, if you have been approved for the credit requested and it is determined that you submitted

## Tracking Credit Applications Worksheet

| Creditor's Name & Address | Date Application Mailed | Approved Date | Declined: Date & Reason |
|---|---|---|---|
| | | | |
| | | | |
| | | | |
| | | | |
| | | | |
| | | | |
| | | | |
| | | | |
| | | | |
| | | | |
| | | | |
| | | | |
| | | | |
| | | | |
| | | | |
| | | | |
| | | | |
| | | | |
| | | | |
| | | | |
| | | | |
| | | | |
| | | | |
| | | | |
| | | | |
| | | | |
| | | | |

information that was not correct, the creditor can cancel your line of credit on the basis of fraud.

## Cost of Credit

When you make a purchase on the basis of a loan or your credit cards, an APR is charged for the use of the money. To calculate the total cost of a loan, multiply your monthly payments by the total number of months. Subtracting the total amount borrowed from the total monthly payments will show you how much interest you've paid for the use of the money. For example: You bought a car with a loan for $8,500; your payment is $240 a month for four years (48 months).

```
$    240  payment per month        $11,520  payments
    × 48  months                  –  8,500  loan
 $11,520  total payments made      $ 3,020  interest paid
```

It is important to know how much you are spending for interest on any purchase.

For a credit card, some banks will calculate interest on a daily basis, while banks that issue other credit cards calculate interest on a prorated interest. A prorated interest means no interest is charged until the billing cycle. If the balance is paid off before the billing cycle, no interest is charged. Paying the balance off before the billing cycle ends is always the best way to use credit.

If the balance on a credit card purchase is not paid off by the end of the billing period, the interest (or finance charge) is added to the balance.

The Sample Credit Card Chart indicates what you'll be paying if you only pay the minimum amount of your payment each month. Notice the total interest you would pay and the total number of months it would take to pay off the beginning balance. The amounts shown are for balances that no other charges would reflect.

REMEMBER! As the balance decreases, so does the minimum pay-ment.

## Sample Credit Card Chart

| Balance | Number of Months Until Paid | Total Interest Paid |
|---|---|---|
| $5,000 | 266 | $6,704.63 |
| 4,900 | 265 | 6,564.62 |
| 4,800 | 263 | 6,424.65 |
| 4,700 | 261 | 6,284.62 |
| 4,600 | 260 | 6,144.62 |
| 4,500 | 258 | 6,004.65 |
| 4,400 | 256 | 5,864.64 |
| 4,300 | 254 | 5,724.63 |
| 4,200 | 252 | 5,584.62 |
| 4,100 | 250 | 5,444.61 |
| 4,000 | 249 | 5,304.61 |
| 3,900 | 246 | 5,164.61 |
| 3,800 | 244 | 5,024.62 |
| 3,700 | 242 | 4,884.63 |
| 3,600 | 240 | 4,744.64 |
| 3,500 | 238 | 4,604.65 |
| 3,400 | 236 | 4,464.62 |
| 3,300 | 233 | 4,324.63 |
| 3,200 | 231 | 4,184.64 |
| 3,100 | 228 | 4,044.63 |
| 3,000 | 226 | 3,904.62 |
| 2,900 | 223 | 3,764.65 |
| 2,800 | 220 | 3,624.64 |
| 2,700 | 217 | 3,484.63 |
| 2,600 | 214 | 3,344.63 |
| 2,500 | 211 | 3,204.64 |
| 2,400 | 209 | 3,064.65 |
| 2,300 | 205 | 2,924.61 |
| 2,200 | 201 | 2,784.65 |
| 2,100 | 197 | 2,644.63 |
| 2,000 | 193 | 2,504.62 |
| 1,900 | 189 | 2,364.62 |
| 1,800 | 185 | 2,224.65 |
| 1,700 | 180 | 2,084.61 |

## Sample Credit Card Chart

| Balance | Number of Months Until Paid | Total Interest Paid |
|---|---|---|
| 1,600 | 176 | 1,944.63 |
| 1,500 | 171 | 1,804.61 |
| 1,400 | 165 | 1,664.65 |
| 1,300 | 159 | 1,524.64 |
| 1,200 | 153 | 1,384.64 |
| 1,100 | 146 | 1,244.65 |
| 1,000 | 138 | 1,104.63 |
| 900 | 130 | 964.65 |
| 800 | 121 | 824.62 |
| 700 | 110 | 684.65 |
| 600 | 98 | 544.63 |
| 500 | 83 | 404.64 |
| 400 | 65 | 264.61 |
| 300 | 43 | 129.11 |
| 200 | 25 | 48.32 |
| 100 | 12 | 10.89 |

Figures are based on minimum payment of 3 percent of balance and 1.75 percent interest per month; may vary by bank.

## Mortgages

Purchasing a house is probably one of the largest investments a person may ever make. Many people, when deciding to purchase a home, have no idea what a lender or mortgage company will look for to qualify them for a loan.

### The Application

The type of loan you apply for determines the amount of your down payment. No matter what type of loan you apply for, the lender will assess you on the basis of certain criteria. You must therefore fill out numerous forms such as the initial loan application, verification of employment, and verification of deposit.

Your loan application requires information about you and your spouse or your coborrower. A coborrower is someone who is purchasing the property with you and helps you qualify for the loan; a coborrower may be your parents, for example, or an unrelated individual.

The loan application is similar to a financial statement and must be filled out completely. Be sure to list all of your assets: all the property you own, cars, furniture, jewelry, silver, and so on. Mention anything that adds to your net worth. After you've listed your liabilities (or debts you owe), usually the lender won't consider any debts that will be paid off within the next ten months.

Again, be aware of details on your credit reports. If you have had problems in the past with credit, it is best to tell the lender in advance about them. Lack of communication leads to denials of loan applications. Occasionally a letter of explanation may be all that is required regarding a negative item that is on your report. It's easier to get a home loan in most cases than to get a credit card because the house itself is the security for the mortgage.

**Past bankruptcy.** If you've had a past bankruptcy, you could still qualify for a new loan if the bankruptcy has been discharged for two years or more and new credit has been established. A good credit history must be established after the bankruptcy with no new derogatory information listed.

Professional Credit Counselors can assist you in analyzing your credit situation and help you get a refinancing or a new mortgage. Call or write Professional Credit Counselors, 1100 Irvine Blvd., #541, Tustin, CA 92780; 714-541-2637.

## Verification of Employment

The lender will send a verification of employment form to your employer for confirmation of where you work. The form contains a questionnaire for your employer or another authorized person to complete. Questions are asked about the length of your employment, your base amount of pay per hour (or monthly), your overtime pay, bonuses, and commissions. Lenders want loan applicants to have been employed for at least two years at the same job. Being employed, for example, for two months at a new job but employed with another company prior to that one and doing the same type of work is considered an acceptable length of employment. The lender will also send a verification of employment form to any other employer you've had within the past two years. Any time applicants change jobs to better themselves financially, lenders are satisfied. But when applicants have a break in employment for several months or quit several jobs and show no stability, then lenders raise questions. They may ask for a letter of explanation or possibly reject the loan. Every lender has different criteria for approving loans.

## Verification of Deposit

The verification of deposit form is mailed to the bank (or banks) that the applicant has indicated as the source of the down payment. The bank must fill out the form to show the applicant's balance and average daily balance. The bank then returns the form to the mortgage company. When you apply for a loan for a house, the loan company doesn't allow you to borrow money for your down payment or closing costs. If you're short the down payment, occasionally the lender will allow a relative to loan you the money if the relative writes a letter or signs a statement indicating the money is a gift and does not have to be repaid. This is called a *gift letter.*

## The Appraisal

One important part of the loan package is the appraisal on the property. At the beginning of this process, while you're filling out a loan application, the lender will ask for a check to cover your credit report fee and appraisal fee, both of which are nonrefundable. The lender then assigns an appraiser to look at the property you want, comparing it to other homes in the area; and a market study is done to determine the value of the property. It is hoped that the property will be appraised at or near the selling price. If the property's appraisal is lower than its sales price, the bank will loan only a percentage of the appraised value and the applicant-purchaser may pay more than the appraised value or renegotiate with the seller. If the seller doesn't wish to renegotiate, the buyer isn't obligated to complete the sale because the sale was based on the original sales price. If the property is appraised for more than the sales price, the original sales price remains the same and the lender will base the down payment on the selling price. Very seldom is a property appraised for more than the sales price because the appraiser knows what the sales price is before making the appraisal.

## The Total Package

After the credit reports, verification of employment, verification of deposits, and appraisal are received by the lender, the loan package is then ready to be submitted to the underwriter (the loan company) for final approval.

A good rule to use in qualifying for your house payment is the four-to-one method, meaning your monthly payment does not exceed four times your monthly gross. For example, if your house payment is $400 per month, then your gross monthly income should be $1,600. Every lender uses a different ratio, however, so be sure to discuss the ratio with the lender at the time you apply.

## Refinancing Your Home

Refinancing a home requires the same process as qualifying for a loan. Many lenders, in doing a refinance, have different types of programs. Second trust deeds or equity lines of credit to take cash out can be 100 percent to 125 percent of the appraised value.

Many people refinance their home to lower their payments and interest rates. Some refinance their home to pay off their debts (credit cards), which saves them money and long-term high interest charges.

Contact Professional Credit Counselors to assess your situation and help you get a loan and reorganize your debts.

# Chapter 5

# Resist the Urge!

## Exercising Control

Using credit can be enjoyed by consumers who keep their credit buying under control. Most people can afford to devote 10 percent of their net income to installment debt, not including mortgage payments. If you pay out more than 15 percent, you should cut back; if more than 20 percent, serious financial trouble can result.

## Control Your Spending

To avoid becoming overextended, use the Credit Control Worksheet to keep a record of your credit debts; complete it each month and examine any increases.

Do not accept or keep more credit than you need. Keep a $500 to $2,000 reserve of unused credit for emergencies. Unused credit is counted against you when you apply for a loan or other credit. Don't expand your credit when you receive a raise; inflated costs and taxes seldom leave much surplus for increased spending.

Keep your credit cards to a minimum. I suggest that you carry no more than three cards because the more you have, the greater the urge to overspend. In addition, revolving accounts carry lower interest rates on amounts over $500, so keeping $1,000 on one card is cheaper than $500 each on two cards.

## Are You an Overspender?

(Answer true or false)

1. I spend money on the expectation that my income will rise.

2. I take cash advances on credit cards to make payments on another credit card.

3. I spend over 20 percent of my income on credit card bills.

4. I often fail to keep an accurate record of my purchases.

5. I have applied for more than three credit cards in the past year.

6. I regularly pay for groceries with a credit card because I have to.

7. I often hide my credit card purchases from my family.

8. Owning several credit cards makes me feel richer.

9. I like to collect cash from friends in restaurants, then pay the bill with my credit card.

10. I almost always make only the minimum payment on my credit card bill.

11. I have trouble imagining life without credit.

**Scoring**
More than TWO true answers: YOU MUST STOP!
It's time to draw up a budget, pay off bills, and reevaluate your spending.

## Minimum Charges

Never charge any item under $25 if you don't intend to pay off the charge at the end of the month. A significant portion of consumer debt stems from small purchases that probably never would have been made if the consumer would have paid cash. Why should you pay interest on a small debt for several years if you could have paid in cash at the time of your purchases?

Always figure out how much it will take to repay your loans with interest. Shop for loans to determine the best rates available. Bring the

# Personal Budget Worksheet

Month _____

Complete this form every month to determine your use of expenditures.

|  | Projections | Actual |
|---|---|---|
| **Income** | | |
| Salaries | _____ | _____ |
| Wages from self-employment | _____ | _____ |
| Dividends | _____ | _____ |
| Interest | _____ | _____ |
| Rental | _____ | _____ |
| Capital gains | _____ | _____ |
| Other | _____ | _____ |
| **Total Income** | _____ | _____ |
|  | | |
| **Fixed Expenses** | | |
| Food | _____ | _____ |
| Housing | _____ | _____ |
| Utilities | _____ | _____ |
| Transportation | _____ | _____ |
| Maintenance | _____ | _____ |
| Furnishings | _____ | _____ |
| Clothing | _____ | _____ |
| Installment purchases | _____ | _____ |
| Personal care | _____ | _____ |
| Insurance premiums | _____ | _____ |
| Medical & dental care | _____ | _____ |
| Education | _____ | _____ |
| Taxes (federal, state, local) | _____ | _____ |
| Other | _____ | _____ |
| **Total Fixed Expenses** | _____ | _____ |

---

## Personal Budget Worksheet (Continued)

| | Projections | Actual |
|---|---|---|
| **Total Available Income** | | |
| (Subtract income from fixed expenses) | | |
| Variable expenses | _____ | _____ |
| Entertainment | _____ | _____ |
| Recreation | _____ | _____ |
| Vacations | _____ | _____ |
| Investments | _____ | _____ |
| Other | _____ | _____ |
| **Total Variable Expenses** | _____ | _____ |
| **Balance for Reserve** (total available income minus variable expenses) | _____ | _____ |

---

figures home and make your determination there, never in the lender's office. By being concerned about your debts you can make credit work for you.

## Handling Credit Problems before They Start

Credit is extended for two reasons. The first is to increase sales; merchants know that more sales will be made when the need for ready cash is eliminated. The second is to make money; stores, banks, and finance companies make a profit from the interest they charge.

Before you are issued credit, two factors are used to determine your "creditworthiness." First, your ability to repay your debts is determined by your job, the length of your employment and position, and the like. Second, your past credit is examined, including which creditors have issued you credit, the amount issued, and your repayment history.

Credit managers usually estimate your net income at 80 percent of your gross income (before taxes). Your committed expenses (rent, bills, etc.) should not exceed 70 percent of your net income. Variable

## Credit Control Worksheet

Month _____

Current Credit Obligations:

| Name of Creditor | Amount Owing | Monthly Payment |
|---|---|---|
| _____ | _____ | _____ |
| _____ | _____ | _____ |
| _____ | _____ | _____ |
| _____ | _____ | _____ |
| _____ | _____ | _____ |
| _____ | _____ | _____ |
| _____ | _____ | _____ |
| _____ | _____ | _____ |
| _____ | _____ | _____ |
| _____ | _____ | _____ |
| _____ | _____ | _____ |
| _____ | _____ | _____ |
| _____ | _____ | _____ |
| _____ | _____ | _____ |
| Grand Monthly Total | _____ | _____ |
| Net Income (personal budget sheet) | | _____ |
| Maximum Credit Payments (10% of net income) | | _____ |

expenses, such as food, fuel, utilities, and so on, are estimated to be about 20 to 25 percent of your net income. Credit managers prefer to see only about 90 to 95 percent of your net income committed to all expenses. If you exceed these figures, you are probably overextended on your credit.

Credit history is considered to be more important than your ability to repay any credit extended. The best references are major bank cards, travel and entertainment cards, and major department store cards.

These cards reflect major purchasing power. Steady repayment over time is considered the ideal credit condition. It reflects a good payment pattern that in turn is reported on your credit report. Home and auto loans are considered to reflect your basic financial strength. Credit extended within the past three years is the most reliable indication of credit ability. Credit managers favor amounts and terms similar to those you have previously repaid. To obtain a favorable credit history, you need several open accounts, which is not to say you need to be in debt.

By having open accounts, you can repay the balances owed at the end of the month to show a good payment pattern. That is always the best method of payment in case an emergency occurs that will affect your finances.

It is essential that you know what your credit report says about you. If you don't, you may be surprised, as I've said several times, at the inaccurate information that may appear. It can happen to anyone.

Credit problems result from a lack of communication between the consumer and the creditor. Not all credit problems are the responsibility of the consumer; lost mail, delayed posting of payments, and clerical/computer errors are the most common credit problems blamed on the creditor. Unreported changes of address, underpayment, missed payments, and the overextension of credit are cited as the prevalent reasons consumers develop credit problems.

Keep your address current with each creditor; notify each creditor before moving to a new address. Complete a change of address form and file it with the post office. Watch for any change of address forms in your monthly statements and report your new address.

If unforeseen circumstances make it impossible to make your full monthly payment, pay as much as possible. Explain by letter or phone the problem and devise a repayment schedule compatible with both your needs. Most creditors are willing to do that to retain you as a customer.

If your accounts have gotten so badly out of control and creditors are threatening to turn you over to a collection agency, work out a plan with them to repay the balance. Ask them to remove any negative items showing on your credit report so long as you do your part to repay the bill. Have the creditors send you in writing a statement that they will remove all negative items upon receipt of the payment. Be sure to keep your end of the agreement.

When an account is turned over to a collection agency, make some effort to settle the account. Many times you can negotiate what is owed; for example, if you have an outstanding bill for $500, offer to pay $350 in full and have the agency agree to remove the entry from your credit report. If the agency refuses to remove the entry, have them show the account as paid in full with no outstanding balance. Partial payment is better than no payment at all. Many times a collector will negotiate, so give it a try, but be firm!

## The Risk of Cosigning for a Loan

A biblical proverb says, "A man lacking in judgment strikes hands in pledge and puts up security for his neighbor" (Prov. 17:18 NIV).

Many young adults with no credit history have their parents cosign or guarantee loans. Other borrowers who seek friends or relatives as co-signers may have had serious credit problems in the past and cannot qualify for a loan. Cosigning a loan can be a high risk if cosigners don't understand what they are doing before making the commitment.

On numerous occasions I have had clients come to my office upset and confused because a negative entry was placed on their credit report from a creditor for whom they were a cosigner. They didn't realize they had any liability on the financed item if it was not paid as agreed.

Frequently, cosigners are the last to know of any problems in repaying a loan they cosigned. When a creditor tries and fails to collect money from the primary borrower, the cosigner is then notified.

It is important that a cosigner knows what to expect before signing any guarantees.

### *What to Expect*

The Federal Trade Commission's (FTC) Credit Practices Rule requires that cosigners be given the following notice:

FTC Notice to Cosigners

You are being asked to guarantee this debt. Think carefully before you do so. If the borrower does not pay the debt, you will be required to pay the debt. Be sure you can afford to pay if you must, and that you want to accept this responsibility.

You may have to pay up to the full amount of the debt if the borrower does not pay. You may also have to pay late fees or collection costs, which increase this amount.

The creditor can collect this debt from you without first trying to collect from the borrower. The creditor can use the same collection methods against you that can be used against the borrower, such as suing you, garnishing your wages, etc. If this debt is ever in default, that fact may become a part of your credit record.

When you cosign for a loan, you'll be required to complete a credit application. The information you supply to the creditor is the basis for its decision for approval. By completing the credit application, you are giving the creditor permission to check your credit report and credit references. You are also agreeing to allow the creditor to report all payment history on this account to the credit bureaus.

When you cosign for a loan, just as when you guarantee a loan, you promise the lender that you'll pay if the primary applicant doesn't. Information on the payment history is reported on both the applicant and the cosigner. The loan amount is also reported and will increase your debt liability. If your payments are delinquent, your credit report will reflect it.

Make sure the primary applicant lets you know if he or she is going to be late making a payment. You may choose to make the payment to safeguard your credit rating. Review your credit report periodically to make sure the payments are being made on time.

## Using Credit to Make Money

Credit cards can make money for you if used wisely. The main thing to remember is to never charge anything on your credit cards that you cannot pay back. By following the procedures in this book, you should be able to obtain several Visa and MasterCard cards.

I usually recommend that you use only one or two credit cards for living expenses and shopping. Select two department stores where you enjoy shopping and use only their cards; and use your gas and oil credit cards as needed. The number of Visa and MasterCards you collect is up to you and your qualifications. The key is to pay off the balance of these cards at the end of each month.

## Investments

The way to make money with your credit cards is by investing. Know the value of a good deal. See where you can make a profit with someone else's money. There are tremendous benefits in careful strategies.

Here's an example: Suppose you found a house you'd like to purchase but don't have the down payment. You can handle this situation two ways. First, find out if the loan is an assumable loan, whereby if the property is appraised at $120,000, you offer the seller $90,000 and assume the existing balance of $70,000, leaving a difference of $20,000 in cash that is needed to assume the existing balance. You have no ready cash, but you have 20 unused Visa and MasterCard cards. Each of these cards has a $2,000 credit limit, allowing you a total of $40,000 in cash advances. By taking 10 of your credit cards to a local bank and collecting $20,000 in cash, you now have the down payment money to complete the purchase of the house. Remember! You can go to any bank or savings and loan to get a cash advance as long as it accepts Visa and MasterCard cards. It does not have to be the bank or savings and loan that issued your credit cards.

The property you want has an appraised value of $120,000, and you bought it for $90,000. With the $70,000 you owe, you have $50,000 in equity. If you wanted to draw your cash out, you could have a second deed of trust placed on the property, get an equity line of credit, or completely refinance the house with a new loan. (Check with your state to see if these types of loans are available and verify if they have any restrictions.)

Many banks will loan from 80 to 90 percent of a house's appraised value. Using the 80 percent loan figure and an appraisal value of $120,000, approximately $26,000 in cash can be taken out with $24,000 in equity remaining.

Using figures on the basis of a 90 percent assumable new loan, you would be able to take out $38,000 in cash and still have $12,000 in equity remaining. You should use the cash you withdraw to repay the $20,000 credit card balances and keep the remainder as your profit. You could use this same procedure and pay all cash for the house if you had that much in cash advances available. You then could refinance the property for whatever amount you wanted.

Remember, the above illustration is beneficial only if you realize a profit and the credit card debts are repaid. Interest charges on the cards accrue during the time of refinancing, so be prepared to include those charges on your pay-off balance.

Before completing any property purchase for which you plan to draw cash from your credit cards, have a lender prequalify you to make sure you can obtain the loan you need. Also, have the lender give you an estimate of all your closing costs.

Investments come in many sizes, shapes, and forms. By knowing market conditions and values, you can profit handsomely from using cash advances through your credit cards.

## Distress Sales

Distress sales on cars, antiques, jewelry, land, and housing can make money for you if you invest the money wisely.

If, for example, you see a car for sale for $3,500 but know it's worth $5,000, use your credit card's cash advance to buy it. Then put the car up for sale yourself for $5,000 and, if you're successful, you've made a $1,500 profit. (Be sure to pay off the credit card debt.) If you complete the transaction within the grace period of your credit card (which is usually 25 days), you'll have no interest charge to pay.

Look for deals you can turn around for profit within your credit card's grace period. By doing this, you'll have had the use of money without any charge.

Newspapers, pennysavers, home mailers, and various bulletin boards, for example, are resources for finding profitable deals.

## Final Comment

The purpose of the preceding chapters has been to enlighten you about obtaining credit. If you follow the suggestions, you should be able to obtain credit.

Use your credit wisely. Be cautious. Never charge anything under $25. If you can't pay for it, don't charge it. There is no sense in paying interest for something you can't afford.

Pay your credit cards off promptly to make yourself more credit-worthy. Be responsible in your charging. Look for ways to make money. It's easy to do as long as you are disciplined with what you have.

Do your homework when applying for credit. Learn everything there is to know about credit. BE AN EXPERT!

# Part Two

# Dealing
# with Credit
# Problems

# Chapter 6

# Who's Watching Me?
## Dealing with Credit Problems

## Credit Problems

The telephone rings and Brenda's heart begins to pound. Is it another bill collector calling to demand payment? The letters from her creditors demanding her past due payments never stop coming. She lives in constant fear and torment imagining the worst is going to happen to her and her family. When his company downsized, Brenda's husband lost his job. The couple had had a good income, were paying all their bills, and had an excellent rating on their credit report. Now everything was changed. The bills could not be paid, there was only enough money for living expenses, and the stress and tension in their home was overbearing.

Money problems have a way of causing instability and turmoil in a marriage, a family, and a home. The pressure is more than most people can handle. A feeling of helplessness can consume an individual who is facing money problems. Brenda is one of many individuals facing money and credit problems in the United States, a common occurrence today.

Credit problems can be devastating. Once they begin, it seems as though there is no hope, but knowing how to deal with these problems can ease the pressure from your creditors.

## Knowledge: The Key to Peace

Knowledge will help you deal with problems involving money and credit instead of waiting until it's too late. Knowing what you can do to stop creditors' harassment will be explained in future chapters as well as defining what bankruptcy really is.

Everyone from time to time will be faced with financial disruption. The main thing to remember is to not panic. Keeping a clear mind and solving the problem is your main goal. Don't let creditors and institutions intimidate you. Learn what your options are and plan your strategies to correct the situation.

## Notifying Creditors

Nothing is more frustrating and upsetting than falling behind in your monthly obligations because of divorce, illness, or losing your job. The main thing is to try to stay calm. Immediately notify your creditors of the problems you're facing. If you let them know before you are delinquent, the chances are better that they will work with you. They're not out to "get you" or cause you mental distress; they're only doing their job in trying to collect their debts. They don't know you personally so don't take it personally. By letting them know your situation, they usually will work with you if they believe it is only a temporary arrangement. Too often consumers wait until they are one or two months late in their payments before they get in touch with creditors even though they've received past due notices and calls regarding their accounts. By calling or writing to creditors at the beginning of your problem to let them know your situation, you have a better chance of working out a solution.

Occasionally, you can negotiate with a creditor to pay a reduced amount of the bill. For example, if your payment is $50 a month, ask if you can pay $25 a month until you can resume making regular payments. Depending on what type of loan or credit you have, a creditor will occasionally extend the debt's repayment period. For example, for a 36-month term, a creditor may add one or two payments to the end of the term, making the term 37 or 38 months. Many car loan companies will defer one payment once a year. Sometimes an "interest only" payment will satisfy a creditor. It doesn't hurt to ask to see what creditors can do to assist you.

If you're dealing with a collection agency, offer to pay one-third or even more in exchange for a cancellation of the debt. Surprisingly enough, the collection agency may go along with your offer. A more detailed discussion of collection agencies can be found in Chapter 7.

If you are in desperate need for assistance, make an appointment with your local Consumer Credit Counseling Service, a nonprofit organization that you can locate in the white pages of the telephone directory. More details about this organization are in a later section of this chapter.

If you see no hope in your situation, phone an attorney who can inform you of, and explain, your options.

## *Overcoming Fear*

The most important thing to remember is to not let fear and intimidation consume you. If you are fearful, make a list of the things you fear will happen (see the Face Your Fear Worksheet). While going through this list, ask yourself, If the worst possible thing did happen:

- Would I lose my health?
- Would I lose my life?
- Would I lose my family?
- Would I lose my friends?

After you've answered these questions, your worst fears shouldn't look so grim. Money can't fix everything, but it does make life more tolerable even if it can't buy health, life, family, or friends.

The more prepared you are to deal with your problems, the better equipped you'll be for a solution. Fears are felt by everyone, especially about problems involving money. Try to put these fears in proper perspective to set a plan of action.

## Know Your Priorities

When dealing with money and credit problems, it is essential to know what your priorities are. If your income has dropped substantially and your savings have been depleted, there's no way you can pay all your credit card charges, loans, and living expenses: the money just won't stretch to every creditor. When your money has run out, *survival* is the key. Having a roof over your head, food on the table, electricity, gas, and

## ✎ Face Your Fear Worksheet

By writing down your greatest fears, you'll be able to handle your problems more effectively. List those fears. Ask yourself: Will I lose my health? Will I lose my life? Will I lose my family? Will I lose my friends?

_____

_____

_____

_____

_____

_____

_____

_____

_____

_____

_____

_____

_____

_____

If you answer no to these questions, what are you afraid of?

a telephone must be your priorities. Don't wait until your money is depleted and nothing can be paid; make a plan before that happens. The damage on your credit report has already been done.

When setting a plan of action to repay your bills, know which ones must be paid immediately and which will have to be paid at a later date. You need to know the consequences you face by not paying each of your debts; and the consequences are usually different from each creditor. If the consequence is severe, you should try to pay the debt. That is categorized as an *essential debt*. If the consequence is not too severe and you can pay the debt at a later time, categorize it as a *nonessential debt*.

## Essential Debts

An essential debt is one that you need to rate as a high priority. The following sections describe those debts that are obviously essential and must be included when structuring a scheduled monthly plan.

**Rent or mortgage payments.** Payments for your rent or mortgage should be your number one priority even though they may be too high for you. If you're renting, try to look for another house or apartment with cheaper rent. Analyze your housing situation when your financial problem first occurs. If you wait too long, it will be more difficult to move because, with your money depleted, you won't have the first month's rent and security deposit needed to relocate.

If you own your home and are making mortgage payments that are too high for you, consider selling your home. Use the money from the sale to rent a house with an affordable payment. The rest of the money you have from the sale can then be used to pay other essential bills and save as a reserve until you regain financial security.

Selling your home may not be your answer. You can try to get a second mortgage or a home equity line of credit. That may solve your problem temporarily, but if you fall behind in making your payments on either type of loan, you could lose your home.

**Utility bills.** It is essential that you have electricity, heat, water, and a telephone. You could live without cable television, but the other items are necessities for survival.

If you're having trouble making utility payments when they're due, phone each utility company and make arrangements for installment payments. The companies are usually willing to work with you, and may even have special programs available for assistance. Ask each company's customer service representative about any such program.

**Car payments.** If you need your car to go to work, try to keep your car payments current. You risk repossession if you don't. Most car loans are secured by the car itself, so if the payments aren't made, the creditor can repossess the car to repay the loan. In most cases the creditor will sell the car for less than you owe and you'll then owe the creditor the difference.

By selling your car and paying it off, however, you'll be able to protect your credit rating. You could also use the money you have left over

## Essential Debt Worksheet

Complete this worksheet by writing in the names of the creditors whom you owe and the amount of the monthly payments. Remember that essential debts are those that *must* be paid.

**Creditor Name**                                    **Amount**

Mortgage _____

Rent _____

Electric co. _____

Gas co. _____

Telephone co. _____

Car payment _____

Secured loans _____

_____

_____

_____

Medical needs _____

Child support _____

Unpaid taxes _____

Other _____

_____

_____

_____

_____

to purchase a cheaper car requiring a lesser payment. A repossession showing on your credit report hurts your chances of financing another car in the future.

**Secured loans.** Secured debts are items that are used as security or collateral to obtain a loan. A secured item is a guarantee that if payments aren't made, the item will be returned to the creditor; it can be furniture, a car, a boat, a recreational vehicle, a house, or anything similar that was pledged as security. After determining what items you have that are secured, ask yourself if you're willing to have creditors take any items back for nonpayment. If you don't care, then let the creditors take them back. If you feel you cannot live without a particular item, then arrange to make the payments. Don't risk losing the item.

**Medical needs.** If you have medical insurance and also medical problems, you'd be taking too big a risk to let the policy lapse. Once the policy lapses and you've had a previous medical problem, you will have trouble getting a new policy.

Whether you have medical insurance or not, you must not let your health deteriorate. Get medical help. By taking care of any medical problems in the beginning, you have a better chance of recovery. Remember: You cannot work if you're sick.

**Child Support.** You can go to jail for not paying child support. If your income has dropped, you may be eligible, however, for a reduction of your child support obligation. I usually suggest that you seek the advice of an attorney to determine your eligibility.

**Unpaid taxes.** The Internal Revenue Service (IRS) and state revenue departments may take your paycheck (garnish your wages), attach your bank accounts, and place a lien on your house or other property to pay any back taxes you owe. It is important that you make arrangements for repayment. Call the IRS and your state's revenue department to make payment arrangements. Don't wait for them to call you.

## Nonessential Debts

Debts for which you will not suffer severe consequences or immediate effects if you don't pay them right away are considered nonessential debts. Your main goal should be to eventually pay off these debts, but they are not a top priority on your list. They can be set aside for a later date if you are unable to pay right now. Some nonessential debts are discussed below.

**Credit and charge cards.** Most credit and charge cards are unsecured because nothing is pledged as security to creditors to guarantee payment. If you fall behind on your payments, the worst that would happen is that the creditor would close your account and perhaps sue you. Each

## Nonessential Debt Worksheet

Complete this worksheet by writing in the names of the creditors whom you owe and the amount of the monthly payments. Remember that nonessential debts are ones that won't lead to severe consequences immediately if put off for a short time.

**Creditor Name**                                                    **Amount**

Credit and charge cards _____

_____

_____

_____

Department store cards _____

_____

Gasoline cards _____
Unsecured loans _____

_____

_____

Loans from friends and relatives _____
Attorney, medical, and accounting bills _____

_____

Newspaper and magazine subscriptions _____
Other _____

_____

_____

_____

creditor has its own policies; some write off an unpaid account as a loss and never pursue it. Most creditors report your nonpayment on your credit report as a negative rating: a charge-off, a collection account, or the number of days your account was delinquent. Most creditors don't report your account delinquent the first month you're late. Find out from each creditor when it reports a delinquent account to the credit reporting agencies.

If you need a credit card for business or personal use, select one card and pay the minimum amount due on that one. If you keep just one card, then it becomes essential and a priority debt.

**Department store and gasoline charge cards.** Credit from department store and gasoline charge cards is not secured. The worst thing that would happen to you from nonpayment is a negative credit rating, your credit line closed, and a possible lawsuit by the creditor.

Because most gasoline stations and department stores offer credit and take charge cards, you can use the one card you have saved for the future.

**Loans from friends and relatives.** Sometimes loans from friends and relatives are the most painful, especially if you are unable to pay them back when you planned. If you can't, explain the situation to each person and hope each is understanding.

**Attorney, medical, and accounting bills.** Attorneys, doctors, and accountants are creditors who can be paid at a later time or with whom you can try to set up payment arrangements.

**Newspaper and magazine subscriptions.** These can be canceled and paid at a later date.

**Unsecured loans.** An unsecured loan has no item pledged for repayment. Finance companies, banks, and savings and loan associations issue unsecured loans. If you quit making payments, their only recourse for repayment is a lawsuit and obtaining a court judgment.

## Borderline Debts

A borderline debt can be either essential or nonessential; and you're the only one who can make that determination. Not paying a borderline debt will not have any severe consequences in your life, although it may cause you anguish.

When trying to decide what is a borderline debt, you need to evaluate how far a creditor has gone in trying to collect on the bill. Many creditors who scream the loudest are not necessarily the most essential to be paid. Some types of borderline debts are reviewed below.

# Borderline Debt Worksheet

Complete this worksheet by writing in the names of the creditors whom you owe and the amount of the monthly payments. Remember that a borderline debt is one that can become either essential or nonessential. Once you have completed your borderline debt entries, transfer them to either the Essential Debt Worksheet or Nonessential Debt Worksheet under "Other."

| Creditor Name | Amount |
|---|---|
| Automobile insurance | |
| Medical insurance | |
| Life insurance | |
| Schools or tutoring | |
| Club memberships | |
| Attorney fees | |
| Clothing | |
| Court judgments | |
| Other | |

**Auto insurance.** Review the type of automobile coverage you have. Talk to your insurance agent to see how your premiums can be reduced. In some states you can lose your drivers license for not having insurance. It is important that you learn what your state requires with regard to automobile insurance. If you let your policy lapse for nonpayment, can you afford the consequences?

When you finance a car through a loan company or bank, your lender will require insurance coverage. If you fail to pay the premium and your policy is canceled, the lender frequently will put its own insurance coverage on the loan, which generally is much more expensive.

**Medical insurance.** Medical insurance is mentioned again as a borderline debt as well as an essential one. Knowing that you have physical problems while letting the policy lapse could be quite serious. You would have a difficult time convincing another insurance company to offer you a policy if you have an existing illness.

On the other side of the coin, if you have no physical problems, you might consider a higher deductible. That would reduce your premium drastically.

If you can't afford medical insurance and let your policy lapse, analyze the consequences.

**Life insurance.** When an individual has financial problems, life insurance is one of first things to lapse. Age is a factor when determining whether to let life insurance lapse. The older you are, the more difficult it is to get a good life insurance policy. The premiums are higher and you must be in good health.

Look at your situation and analyze if a cancellation will benefit you.

**Private schools and outside tutoring for children.** Paying for your child to attend a private school or have outside tutoring may seem unessential. You need to look at the overall picture to see if withdrawing them from a private school or tutoring program will have a lasting effect on their future.

Children are our greatest gifts, and you need to use wisdom when making that decision. If your child needs extra attention in the classroom, then perhaps it is essential that they remain in a private school. If your child has reading or learning problems and needs a tutor, stick with it. Your child's future could be jeopardized.

**Health clubs, gyms, and country clubs.** Belonging to a health club, gym, or country club is generally a luxury. Determine if belonging is essential even if it is hard to give up. Don't let your pride get in the way. Create an alternate. Exercise at home and improve your eating habits for better nutrition. Play golf at a public course. The money you save by resigning from private clubs can be used to pay some essential bills.

**Attorney fees.** If you have had to seek the assistance of an attorney to help with your financial problems and fail to pay for his or her services, you'll be dropped as a client. At that point you'll have to handle your own problems. Can you do that?

**Clothing.** When financial problems occur, it's time to stop shopping in the malls. Learn new ways to shop. Go to garage sales, yard sales, swap meets, and second-hand stores. Young children grow at such a rapid pace that they always seem to need clothing. It is up to you to determine if children's clothes—or yours—are essential or nonessential.

**Court judgments.**  After obtaining a court judgment, a creditor can try to collect unpaid debts by taking a portion of your wages or property. Try to negotiate a payment plan or settlement.

**Other.**  Anything you owe now and are making payments on that has not been mentioned is considered "other." Determine if these other debts are essential or nonessential.

You must decide whether a borderline debt might be essential or nonessential. You must also evaluate which debts are borderline and then determine how to handle the situation you are presently facing.

**Remember!** Never make a payment on a nonessential debt until your essential debts are paid. That is a must. Your survival is the most important thing. If you are facing an eviction or your utilities are going to be turned off, don't pay a credit card bill or anything else that will cause you to be short in paying your essential bills. Pay the nonessential bills only when you have a surplus of money and know that the essentials will be covered monthly.

Facing these decisions and setting a plan of action will help you through a difficult period. Many creditors will use intimidating collection efforts. Stand your ground. A creditor who yells the most is not usually an essential one to pay. Obviously, your intention is to eventually pay off all your debts.

As you complete the debt worksheets, consider carefully what debts you have and divide them into the three categories—essential, nonessential, and borderline—to help you get a clearer picture of where your priorities should be.

## Communicating with Creditors

Communicating with your creditors is probably one of the most difficult things you will have to do when dealing with credit problems. When financial problems occur, it's easy to become overwhelmed and to withdraw from any communication with creditors. By withdrawing, the problems will not go away, and lack of communication with the creditors will only cause more problems for you. Creditors want to be informed of any problems you're facing. The worst thing you can do is cut off communication with creditors. If you do, they will feel that you are ignoring the problem and they may expedite collection efforts.

By communicating with creditors and letting them know what your situation is, you have a better chance of working out a plan for repayment. Much of what can be worked out will depend on the type of debt you have and how far behind you are in making payments. Every creditor has its own policy for delinquent accounts.

## Write or Call

As soon as you realize that you're going to have problems paying your bills, write a letter or call the creditor and explain your situation. It may be loss of a job, emergency expenses for a family member, an accident, a large tax bill, or some other situation that will hamper you in meeting your financial obligations. If at all possible send a small payment to show you are sincere in repaying the debt. This approach applies with both your essential debts and nonessential debts if you have the extra money. A sample letter to send a creditor is shown below.

Sample Letter to Creditor

(Date)

(Company Name)
Re: Account number _____

Dear Company Name,

I am writing in regard to my account with your store. I recently was laid off my job and am in the process of looking for new employment. I have fallen behind with my payments and would like to work out a repayment plan with your company. I am able to pay $10 per month until I am working again. I am enclosing a check for $10 to apply toward my account. Please accept this payment and my proposal for future payments until I am able to fulfill the original terms of my contract.

Sincerely,

John Doe

P.S. Please make this letter a part of my file.

MAIL CERTIFIED MAIL WITH A RETURN RECEIPT

## Negotiate

If your delinquent bills have gotten out of control and a creditor is putting pressure on you for payment, try to negotiate. Negotiating with a creditor can be advantageous to you. Most creditors have a bottom line for what they will take as full payment. There is no set rule on how to negotiate with a creditor. If you are not comfortable doing it yourself, see if a friend or relative will negotiate on your behalf, which can work as long as the negotiator knows what you're able to pay.

A few guidelines when negotiating with a creditor include the following:

- Know what amount you can pay to satisfy the debt. For example, if you have a medical bill of $600 and are unwilling to or can't pay the full amount, offer to pay $400 over a six-month period. If the creditor agrees to this arrangement, get it in writing, making sure the creditor indicates in its letter that when the final payment is received at the end of the six-month period, the account will be satisfied.

- Find out what the creditor's bottom line is for repayment. Many creditors will allow you to make interest-only payments for a limited time. Others may allow you to defer a payment for one month. Some creditors will offer to settle your account, allowing a full payment of up to 50 percent off the balance.

- Many bill collectors or collection agencies will lie to you. If they think you can make a higher payment, they will indicate a certain amount is all they can accept. For example, a collection agency demands a $200 payment but you can't pay that much; tell them what you can pay. If it's only $75, stick with that amount. The agency can take it or leave it. Don't be threatened or bullied into something you cannot afford. The agency will try to make you feel guilty, but don't change your mind. Unforeseen circumstances can happen to anyone, and you can only pay what you have available.

- Determine whether the creditor has a re-aging program, which is a program to set up a new payment schedule. Once you have made the required number of payments to qualify for the program, the account will become current. Request that the creditor report this current activity on your credit report and that no negative entries be shown. For example, Suppose you are six months past due on your credit card payment; the creditor brings your account current after you make three consecutive payments for a specific amount. Any past due payments are dropped, and the account indicates a current status.

The key to negotiating is to follow through with the arrangement you have made. Do exactly what you agreed to do. If you cannot, then notify the creditor immediately and make new arrangements. Stick with your plan. Get a letter from the creditor before you send any money confirming your payment arrangement. Do not send a payment before receiving a confirmation letter from the creditor.

Another thing to remember when negotiating with the creditor is to request removal of any negative entries on your credit report when you have completed your payment arrangement.

There are many different situations for which you may need assistance in negotiating with a creditor. A careful review of the following problem areas may be useful when you are trying to establish a plan to pay your creditors.

**Mortgage payments.** Missing your house payments will cause stress in your life. There is always the possibility of a foreclosure, which can take 6 to 18 months to complete. Keeping this in mind, you can look at several different options that are available. The most obvious would be to sell the house. If you have equity in your home, you could take the money from the sale and rent another home until you are financially stable.

If you have only missed one or two payments, contact your mortgage company to see if a repayment plan can be set up for you. That could be done by giving you, for example, a four-month period to bring the payments current. By adding a portion of your past due payments to the scheduled payments, they would be brought current. For example, if you missed one payment of $800, you would add an additional $200 to your payment, for a total of $1,000 for four months and thus bring the account current.

Some mortgage companies, if notified early enough, may allow you to make interest-only payments and apply the principal to the balance. They may even temporarily reduce or suspend your payments to a later date.

Refinancing your mortgage can be to your advantage only if the payment is considerably lower. The lender you have now may be very accommodating in offering a refinanced mortgage. If you have equity in your home and do refinance, you may have to draw out some of the money to consolidate your bills and/or set aside enough money to make mortgage payments for six months or longer. A lender will evaluate the ratio of your monthly income to your new payment minus your debts. If the ratio is between 25 and 33 percent, you probably will qualify for the new loan.

Another alternative when you're strapped for cash is a second mortgage, which is suggested if your first mortgage already has a low interest rate. Qualifying for a second mortgage draws out enough equity to help you consolidate your bills and avoid a possible foreclosure, but this is advantageous only if you have a stable income and can make the payments. When getting a second mortgage, be sure to read the fine print of the contract. Lenders of second mortgages are usually quicker to react if the payments fall behind. Frequently, a second mortgage is more costly than a first with higher points (a percentage of the amount borrowed that the lender charges) and has a higher interest rate than a first mortgage.

If selling your house, refinancing it, or applying for a second mortgage doesn't work out and the house is in foreclosure, offer the lender a quitclaim deed. A quitclaim deed allows you to deed (or give) the property back to the lender in exchange for cancellation of the debt. The lender gets the property back without going through foreclosure proceedings and you avoid a negative entry on your credit report, thus clearing your name.

**Rent payments.**  Falling behind on your rent payments can lead to your eviction. If you see that your rent payment is going to be late, inform your landlord and explain your problem. If you're going to be only a couple of weeks late paying the rent, the landlord will usually work with you. And if you've been a longtime tenant, the landlord may allow you to make a partial payment and pay the rest later. It's easier for a landlord to keep you than to lose weeks and possibly months of payments while trying to re-rent the house or apartment. If special arrangements have been made, mail a certified letter stating the approved arrangement with a return receipt request. Be fair and pay the rent when you promised.

If you're unable to pay the rent due, look for a cheaper home or apartment. Notify your landlord and make your move.

**Car payments.**   When falling behind with a car payment, you must act quickly to contact the lender. Your car can be repossessed from your missing just one payment. The lender does not really want your vehicle, but it's the only protection for the debt. The longer you're delinquent, the stronger the possibility the car's value will decrease.

Many lenders have their own policies for handling customers who are having financial difficulties. Depending on the number of months the car or vehicle has been financed, some lenders will allow you to defer one payment a year—that is, the payment due for a particular month doesn't have to be made. The deferred payment is added to the end of the contract; so, for example, if your contract was for 36 months, an additional month will be added to make it a 37-month contract.

Some lenders may offer to take interest-only payments on a temporary basis when you're in financial trouble. The difference is added to the end of the contract and is due with the final payment.

If you have been a good customer of the lender's, you might consider refinancing the car to reduce your payments. You would pay longer on the loan, which means more interest payments; however, the pressure would be off of you for the larger payment.

When all else fails and you cannot make the payments, sell the car. Take the money, pay off the loan. Use whatever you have left to purchase another, less expensive car or go without. That is better than having a repossession noted on your credit report, which could prevent you from obtaining a future car loan. Besides ruining your credit report and the chance for future loans, a balance could still be owed after the repossession.

When a company repossesses a car or other vehicle, it will usually sell it for less than is owed on it. The amount the company gets from selling the vehicle is subtracted from the loan amount and the difference is what you still owe and what you're required to pay. Get rid of the car before all that happens.

**Secured loan payments.**   When credit is established by a security agreement pledging such items as furniture, appliances, jewelry, or electronic equipment as collateral, failure to make the payments can result in losing the items that were secured. The lender is not anxious to collect your furniture or other secured items as they depreciate rapidly. The debt, in fact, is usually worth more than the items secured.

A lender cannot enter your home to collect secured items unless it has a court order. The best solution is to negotiate with the lender to rewrite the loan or extend it to reduce your monthly payments.

**Insurance.**   Certain types of insurance may be required in your state or under some of your contracts. *Homeowners* and *automobile insurance,* for example, are required by most lenders. If you don't have these kinds of insurance, companies will insure homes and cars themselves for their own protection; and if they do, the cost is much higher than for standard insurance. Be sure you know the requirements of your contracts as well as those of your state.

*Medical insurance* is essential if you have a medical problem. By letting it lapse, you could have difficulties getting new insurance in the future for a preexisting condition. Call your insurance agent to see if you could raise your deductible: the higher the deductible, the lower the cost of insurance.

If you don't have a medical problem and you let your insurance policy lapse, you probably won't have a problem getting new insurance later on when you're more financially stable.

*Life insurance* is probably a nonessential debt providing you or a family member is not seriously ill. If you let your policy lapse, try to reinstate it at a later time. If you are unable to reinstate it, get a new policy.

Most policies have a 30-day grace period. Thus, if your payment is due on the 15th of the month and you don't pay until the 14th of the following month, you won't lose your coverage. Check with your insurance agent to see what your grace period is.

**Doctor, dentist, accountant, and attorney bills.**   Many doctors, dentists, lawyers, and accountants accept partial payments. Some may reduce their bills rather than send your account to a collection agency if you let them know your financial problems and set up a plan to repay them.

If you need the services of your doctor, dentist, accountant, or lawyer, it would be wise to pay off the old bill as soon as possible.

**Student loans.** You can probably get your student loan deferred if you supply the lender with a letter explaining your financial hardship. If the lender sees that you have a legitimate reason for not paying, it may postpone the payment of the loan. In most instances, however, interest will continue to accrue. Review with your lender its policies for dealing with delinquent student loan accounts.

**Taxes.** If you owe back taxes to either your state or the IRS, it is imperative to set up a repayment plan. When you file your income tax forms in April without enclosing all the money that is due, you'll begin receiving letters from the IRS and your state revenue department asking for the money owed. The letters may start arriving approximately 90 days after you file your tax return. Over the next two to three months, you'll probably receive three or four more computerized letters requesting the amount owed. The last letter you'll receive is certified, demanding the full payment and explaining the consequences of nonpayment. Nonpayment can result in the seizure of your property, which includes attaching bank accounts, garnishing your wages, and putting a lien on your property. Interest and penalties continue to accrue until the taxes are paid in full.

The most important thing is to work out a plan to pay your back taxes to avoid the potentially severe consequences. Don't wait for the IRS to call you.

**Unsecured credit and charge payments.** Most credit card companies require the minimum amount to be paid to keep accounts current. If you don't want to keep an account, then pay it when you have the money to do it.

It is a good idea to keep at least one credit card current if possible. Most merchants require a credit card for identification, as well as for securing a car or reserving a hotel room. Even if you don't use the card, keep it for emergencies as long as you know you can pay it off or at least make the minimum payments.

If you have run into severe financial difficulties, occasionally a creditor will allow you to make a payment of 2 to 3 percent of the outstanding

## Creditor Repayment Worksheet

Month _____

List each creditor to whom you owe money. Include the creditor's name, the minimum payment, the past due amount, balance, and amount you can pay. Do this monthly until you are current.

| Creditor | Minimum Payment | Past Due Amount | Balance | Amount You Can Pay |
|---|---|---|---|---|
|  |  |  |  |  |
|  |  |  |  |  |
|  |  |  |  |  |
|  |  |  |  |  |
|  |  |  |  |  |
|  |  |  |  |  |
|  |  |  |  |  |
|  |  |  |  |  |
|  |  |  |  |  |
|  |  |  |  |  |
|  |  |  |  |  |
|  |  |  |  |  |
|  |  |  |  |  |
|  |  |  |  |  |

balance without a finance charge. Rarely, however, will a creditor waive the interest rate. Something is better than nothing.

Because credit cards are usually unsecured, pay what you can as long as your essential needs are met. Always be open and honest with creditors when discussing your financial problems. They are not out to get you, as I've said before, but are only doing their job in trying to collect a debt.

Many creditors will work with you if you get assistance from a consumer credit counseling program, which will be discussed next.

## Consumer Credit Counseling Service

Consumer Credit Counseling Service (CCCS) is a nonprofit, nation-wide organization affiliated with the National Foundation for Consumer Credit that provides confidential and professional financial counseling.

If you are under stress from credit problems and feel there's nowhere to turn, a CCCS agency is available to assist you in getting your problems solved or to recommend solutions that fit your needs.

When you make an appointment with CCCS, you're requested to bring to the appointment copies of recent pay stubs, outstanding bills, charge account numbers, and copies of letters you've received from creditors. If you're married, it is important that your spouse be present at the initial appointment with the counselor.

At the CCCS office, you will be asked to complete a form detailing your family income, basic living expenses, assets, and details of what you owe.

After reviewing your worksheet, the counselor will determine if there are solutions to your credit problems and will make the necessary recommendations. If the counselor feels you can handle your own problems, he or she will outline a program for you in addition to recommendations. If the problems are too complicated for you to handle by yourself, the counselor will establish a personalized program for repayment to your creditors. The counselor will advise each creditor about your problems and present a brief outline of your financial situation.

Following acceptance of the CCCS plan by the creditors, you will be asked to make fixed payments each month to a personal trust fund at the CCCS office. On receipt of your payment, all creditors are paid on a prorated basis until all your outstanding bills have been paid. On average, the debt management program can last up to 42 months. During that time, your counselor is available to discuss your general financial problems and any emergency problems that may arise.

At the beginning of the prorating program, the creditors are notified of your intention to pay off your debts under a counselor's guidance. Once you have completed the program, new information is added to your credit report. Make sure that the creditors are reporting the activity correctly and that they are not reporting negative information.

Many of the CCCS offices have waiting lists for appointments. If you want assistance from CCCS, refer to the white pages in your telephone directory, or call their national toll-free number, 800-388-CCCS (2227).

## Charge Card Problems

By having credit and using charge cards, you are responsible for the use of the cards and the purchases made with the cards. Even though there may be more than one user of a credit card, the person who initially signed the contractual agreement requesting the card is the one responsible for payment. If you have requested an additional card for your spouse or another party, it is you that is totally responsible for all users and for total payments. If you wish to cancel another cardholder's privileges, you must notify the issuing card company by telephone *and* in writing indicating that you want to cancel the cardholder's card. Take back the card and cut it in half to guard the credit you have.

Several problems can arise with charge cards, so you need to be aware of remedies for those problems.

### Lost or Stolen Cards

Lost or stolen cards, if left unreported to the bank or company that issued them, can cost you thousands of dollars in unauthorized charges. But federal law limits your liability for unauthorized charges. You must notify the card issuer within a reasonable time, generally 30 days after you discover the card has been lost or stolen. Once you have notified the card issuer, you are no longer responsible for any charges. Your personal liability is limited to $50 for unauthorized charges made before notification to the card issuer. Waiting too long to notify the card issuer can be very dangerous because you are liable for all the charges made on the card before notification.

The problem most people have is carrying four or five credit cards. If you keep them in your wallet and the wallet is stolen, the charges, even with the limited liability, could be $200 to $250 at $50 per card. One way to avoid this risk is to not carry all your cards at one time; put them in a safe place when you're not using them.

When you discover that a credit or charge card is lost or stolen, call the customer service department of the card issuer. Most bank card issuers have a 24-hour customer service department. Other card issuers, such as department stores and gasoline companies, may have limited business hours but call them the next business day and be sure to get the name of the person to whom you are speaking. Send a follow-up letter reporting the loss by certified mail with a return receipt requested. Make copies of all your correspondence.

A sample letter to the credit issuer confirming your telephone notice is show below.

---

## Sample Letter to Credit Card Issuer Confirming Lost Card

(Date)

ABC Department Store
22 E. Nostreet
Anytown, CA 99999

ATTN: Customer Service Dept.
    Anne Smith

Dear Ms. Smith:

This is a follow-up letter confirming our telephone conversation, May 12, 19___. At that time I notified you of my credit card being lost. I was on vacation, and my wallet disappeared.

It is my understanding that by telephoning your company I am not liable for any unauthorized charges made on my card from the date on which I reported the card missing by telephone to you.

Sincerely,

Nancy Engle

Make sure you have a list of all your credit and charge cards, the account numbers, and telephone numbers of the issuers. Keep this list in a safe place (see the Credit Card Record Worksheet).

Some companies may report to the credit reporting agencies that your card was lost or stolen, which could appear as derogatory information if you have had a history of paying your account late. If your account is not satisfactory, the issuer may not reissue a card. Although the chances of this happening are slight, be aware of the consequences. On the other hand, it is far better to report the card lost or stolen rather than pay for unwanted charges.

Many banks and credit or charge card companies offer a credit card protection program for approximately $25 a year. Because your liability is only $50 for charges made before you notify the issuer of the lost or stolen card, a protection program may not be worth the investment. But if you're interested, then by all means find out from the card issuers what programs are available.

## Unauthorized Charges

Unauthorized charges can be a problem even if one of your credit or charge cards is not lost or stolen. Friends or relatives have been known to make unauthorized charges with your card. Generally, you are not liable for the bill if you don't know the person who was using your card. But what if you gave your card to your son or daughter and didn't limit the amount that could be charged? Technically, you are liable for any charges that occur unless you had set limits—it would be difficult to convince a card issuer that you were not responsible.

Another problem that can occur with credit or charge cards is credit card fraud. Fraud can occur when someone has gotten access to your credit card or pertinent information from your credit or charge card. Offenders are known to discover—and use—credit card information from discarded carbons or copies used with credit card charges.

Richard had used his credit card at a local restaurant. Several weeks later he received a copy of his statement and saw numerous charges that he knew he didn't make. After he notified the card issuer, further investigation by the card issuer showed that when Richard paid the restaurant bill several weeks before, the carbon copies of the charge slip had not been destroyed. They were thrown in the trash where someone retrieved

## Credit Card Record Worksheet

Complete for your records in case of a lost or stolen card.

| Credit Card Name | Address | Account Number |
|---|---|---|
| | | |
| | | |
| | | |
| | | |
| | | |
| | | |
| | | |
| | | |
| | | |
| | | |
| | | |
| | | |
| | | |
| | | |
| | | |
| | | |
| | | |
| | | |
| | | |
| | | |

them. By transposing the numbers from the carbon receipt and getting Richard's name, the offender was able to charge items fraudulently.

With credit card fraud increasing, many card issuers are supplying stores, restaurants, and the like with charge slips that do not use carbons. When you use your charge card where carbon copies are used, be sure you get the carbons and tear them up to prevent someone else from using your card numbers. You don't want to be a victim, nor do you want to encourage someone else to do something illegal.

Never give your credit card number to a solicitor over the telephone unless you know the company or individual. By freely giving such pertinent information to the wrong person, you can become a victim of credit card fraud. Whenever you order merchandise or anything else over the telephone and charge with your credit card, the operator will ask for the type of card, your name as it appears on the card, the account number, and the expiration date. Having such complete information, a dishonest person can charge items on your account. *Beware! Be cautious!* Always know who is on the other end of the receiver.

## Disputing Credit or Charge Card Purchases

Suppose you purchased a coat from Reed's Department Store and charged it with your Reed's charge card. At home later, you discovered the pockets had two holes, but Reed's refused to replace the coat or give you a refund. You have the right to refuse to pay the bill when it comes due. Had you charged the coat with your Visa or MasterCard card, you could have refused to pay the charge only if you live within 100 miles of the store or reside in the same state.

If you use your credit or charge card to purchase merchandise or service that is defective in some way, you can withhold your payment if certain conditions are met. Under the Fair Credit Billing Act (14 U.S.C. 1666i), withholding payment is allowed if the following four conditions are met:

1. You must first attempt to resolve the problem with the store or company from which you made the purchase.
2. The charge that was made must be for more than $50.
3. You must inform the credit institution of the dispute in writing.
4. The store from which you made the purchase must be located within 100 miles of your residence or within your state.

When you're attempting to resolve a problem with a store or company about a purchase, always document your telephone calls. List the date and the name of the person with whom you spoke. Make notes of your conversation.

If you send a letter to the store or company (which is recommended) outlining the problem, be sure to send it by certified mail with a return receipt requested.

Keep your receipt of the item you're disputing. The price of the item should not be less than $50.

Notify the credit institution that issued your charge card of a dispute for merchandise or service you purchased with the card. If you withhold payment of the disputed amount, the credit institution cannot put any derogatory information on your credit report and cannot report the account as delinquent.

When you write to the credit institution, be sure to attach photocopies of any correspondence that you have had with the store or company you are disputing. Send your letters by certified mail with a return receipt requested.

The credit institution will get in touch with the store to hear its version of the problem. A decision is made after all the factors are reviewed.

## Billing Errors

Every month you should receive a copy of your credit or charge card statement that should show all charges made with your card during that month. It is very important to review your statement every month. Billing errors do occur. If you rely on the credit institution to track your charge activities, you'll never know if errors are being reported. (See and fill out the Credit Card Monthly Statement Worksheet.)

Credit and charge card billing errors, as indicated previously, are governed by the Fair Credit Billing Act. An explanation of your billing rights and finance charges are located on the back of your monthly statement. If you discover an error in your credit or charge card statement, you must immediately write a letter to the institution that issued the card. An error may involve an item you purchased, an item you did not purchase, or not receiving proper credit on a payment you made.

Your letter must be sent within 60 days from the date the statement was mailed (check the postmarked date) and should be sent by certified mail with a return receipt requested. The institution has 30 days from the postmarked date to acknowledge receipt of your letter. At this point the creditor may make the necessary corrections on your account and notify you in writing of the correction. If the creditor thinks you are not correct, it will send you a written explanation and must provide supporting documentation.

## Credit Card Monthly Statement Worksheet

Review your statement from all credit card companies every month. Compare receipts of your purchases with the statement entries.

Month _____

List Receipts

Issuer _____

| Date | Merchant | Description | Charge Amount |
|------|----------|-------------|---------------|
|      |          |             |               |
|      |          |             |               |
|      |          |             |               |
|      |          |             |               |
|      |          |             |               |
|      |          |             |               |
|      |          |             |               |
|      |          |             |               |
|      |          |             |               |
|      |          |             |               |
|      |          |             |               |
|      |          |             |               |
|      |          |             |               |
|      |          |             |               |
|      |          |             |               |
|      |          |             |               |
|      |          |             |               |
|      |          |             |               |

During the time that you're disputing your bill, the creditor cannot report your account delinquent to any credit reporting agency. Neither can it pursue collection activity on the amount you are disputing. A dispute with the creditor regarding an error must not take any longer to settle than a two billing-cycle period (90 days). Be sure to pay the amount owed the creditor for items that are not being disputed to protect your credit rating. *Remember*! The only amount you can withhold is the amount you are disputing.

All correspondence to the creditor should go to the attention of the customer service department. The address should appear on the statement. *Do not* send your letter to the payment center's address as it will only be passed around. Your letter should include your name, address, account number, and an explanation of the error and the amount that you are disputing. If you have any copies of receipts showing the correct amounts of the charge, include photocopies of them in your letter. A sample letter when you find a billing error is shown below.

## Sample Letter for Correcting a Billing Error

Bank Two
3 Any street
Town, CA 22222

(Date)
Attn: Customer Service
Account Number: 1111 222 44444SX

To Whom It May Concern:

I received my statement dated May 18, 19___. There is an error being reported. On April 2, 19___, I purchased two airline tickets from Aerway Airlines from Dallas to California. The amount I paid was $895. My statement, however, is for $985. I am enclosing a copy of my receipt from the airline.

I understand that you will respond to me within 30 days and make the necessary correction.

Sincerely,

John Jones

# Chapter 7

# Help! They're After Me!
## Working with Collection Agencies

There is a difference between an original creditor trying to collect a debt and a collection agency. The original creditor is the business or person who has extended you credit. A collection agency is an outside company hired by the original creditor to collect the debt that is owed.

An original creditor will make every effort to collect a debt, but when it has grown tired and frustrated, it will turn the account over to an outside agency to recover whatever money it can. Before turning an account over, however, the original creditor will first send a number of letters and make frequent telephone calls in an attempt to get paid what it is owed.

People having difficulty paying their bills will only become more upset and frustrated, for the constant calls and letters indicate that whatever they tell a creditor seems to do no good.

If you are in such a situation, the original creditor may give you six months to respond before either turning the account over to an outside collection agency, writing it off as a bad debt (known as a charge-off), or suing you. No matter what the creditor does, the damage has already been done on your credit report.

If a creditor has given up on you, it will probably first hire a collection agency, which contracts with the creditor to receive a high percent of what is owed as its compensation.

Collection agencies have been known to be ruthless in their tactics to collect a bill; it takes a special type of well-trained individual in fact to work for a collection agency. Collectors are screened carefully before being hired to be sure they can "hang on" and wear you down to the point that you repay the debt. A collector uses a script for communication to deal with any objection you may have. They can be rude, insensitive, insulting, and intimidating. It is not uncommon for collectors to threaten to sue you or garnish your wages, or use equally threatening words to scare you into paying.

You must know what your rights are if confronted by a collection agency; lack of knowledge increases your vulnerability and exposes you to more stress than is necessary. You must know how to deal with collectors in order to set up a repayment plan if that's an option for you. If you can't pay your debt, don't let a collector grind you down. Allowing a collection agency to intimidate you into paying money that will reduce what's available for your essential living expenses can be disastrous.

When a collection agency is hired by an original creditor, it must take its instructions from the creditor, which will lay out certain guidelines for the collection agency. The creditor indicates to the collection agency what its bottom line is for repayment. If the creditor indicates that the agency is to collect 100 percent of the debt, than the agency must adhere to the request and cannot take anything less. If the creditor indicates it will take less, then the agency can relay the message to you. In other words, the collection agency cannot agree to any proposal you make unless it gets permission from the original creditor, which is the only party that can initiate a lawsuit against you. An outside collection agency cannot hire an attorney or use one on staff to sue you.

If the collection agency has purchased the debt from the original creditor, then it can collect the debt however it chooses. The majority of collection agencies, however, are hired only to collect a debt and seldom purchase any.

Before September 1977, a consumer could do very little against ruthless tactics used by a collection agency.

## Your Rights

A federal law was enacted in September 1977–the Fair Debt Collection Practices Act–as a protection for consumers against unethical bill collectors. To receive a copy of the act, contact the Federal Trade Commission, which has been given the power to enforce the provisions of the act.

### Summary of the Act

The creation of the Fair Debt Collection Practices Act came about because of "evidence of abusive, deceptive, and unfair debt collection practices that have contributed to the number of personal bankruptcies, to marital instability, to the loss of jobs, and to the invasion of individual privacy."

A bill collector that communicates with any person other than a consumer to get information about the consumer's whereabouts must identify himself and state that he is confirming or correcting the information and can identify his employer only if expressly requested. The bill collector cannot indicate that the consumer owes any debt. Nor can the collector communicate by postcard or use any language or symbol on a mailed envelope indicating he represents a collection agency or that any debt is owed (for example, "Bill Owed! Call Immediately!"). If the bill collector knows the consumer is represented by an attorney, he must communicate only with the attorney, unless the attorney fails to respond within a reasonable period of time.

A bill collector is only allowed to communicate with a consumer at his or her home between 8:00 AM and 9:00 PM unless the consumer tells the collector differently. If the bill collector calls the consumer's place of work, the consumer can tell the bill collector that the employer does not allow personal calls at work. Once the consumer tells the collector to stop calling him or her at work and follows up with a letter, the collector must comply. The letter should be sent by certified mail with a return receipt requested and a copy sent to the Federal Trade Commission. The letter should refer to consumers' rights under the Fair Debt Collection Practices Act.

Without the consumer's consent, a collection agency may not inform anyone else about any past-due bill of the consumer's except for a credit reporting agency, the consumer's attorney, or the consumer.

A consumer may notify a collection agency in writing that he or she refuses to pay the bill or wishes the collection agency to stop further communication. Upon receipt of this letter, the collection agency must stop all communication except to notify the consumer of any final action that will take place.

If you send a letter to a collection agency to ask it to stop communicating with you, it is wise to send it by certified mail with a return receipt. A sample of such a letter is shown below.

## Sample Letter to Collection Agency for Discontinuing Contact

AAC Collection Service
44 W. Marnie St.
Anytown, State, Zip

(Date)
Attn: Mary Lanz
Re: Matthew Ho
Account No. 11-44-872

Dear Ms. Lanz:

Your company has made several telephone calls and sent numerous letters regarding my account at Toby's Department Store. I have indicated to you that I am unable to pay this bill.

This is my formal notice to you to discontinue all further communications with me. I am aware of my rights under the Fair Debt Collection Practices Act.

Sincerely,

Matthew Ho

A collection agency cannot "harass, oppress, or abuse any person in connection with the collection of a debt." The five specific types of outlawed harassment include the following:

1. Using or threatening to use violence or other criminal means to harm the reputation or property of any person
2. Using obscene or profane language to abuse a consumer
3. Publishing a list of consumers who refuse to pay their bills
4. Initiating the telephone to ring with the intention of annoying, abusing, or harassing consumers
5. Making telephone calls without disclosing the caller's identity

## False or Misleading Representations

A collection agency, under the act, cannot intimate to a consumer that it is representing an attorney or a law office. Representing or implying that the nonpayment of any debt will result in arrest, garnishment, attachment, and the like is unlawful if the collection agency does not intend to take legal action. The threat to take any action that cannot legally be taken or that is not intended to be taken is a violation of consumers' rights.

## Payment and Finance Charges

A collection agency cannot add on any finance charges or service fee in collecting a debt unless the extra charge has been authorized and signed by the consumer in the agreement creating the debt. On a bill with a balance of $75, for example, the bill collector cannot add on an extra $15 as a "service fee."

Many times a collection agency requests a postdated check. If a consumer sends checks postdated more than five days prior to the deposit date, the collection agency must send a letter of intent to deposit the check at least three days prior to depositing.

## Your Right to Verify the Debt

Federal law gives you the right to verify any debt you feel is not valid. The collection agency, when notifying you in writing of a debt owed, must include in the notice "the amount of the debt, the name of the creditor to whom the bill is owed, and a statement that unless the consumer, within thirty days after receipt of the notice, disputes the validity of the debt, or any portion of the debt, it will be assumed to be valid by the debt collector." That means you have no recourse if you don't dispute the written request. No response indicates that the bill is in fact owed. However, if you notify the collection agency within 30 days that you are disputing the bill, the collection agency must provide you a verification of the debt and any documentation indicating the debt is owed. During the time before the debt is verified by the collection agency, it can undertake no further collection procedures. Remember, any written correspondence should be sent by certified mail with a return receipt.

## Communicating with Collection Agencies

The initial contact you have with a collection agency is by telephone or letter, neither of which is generally pleasant. The main thing you want to do is remain calm and not let the caller or letter upset you. The collector is only trying to collect the money and will use whatever means it has. The collection agency will try to wear you down and will have a response for anything you say. Remember, the collection agency has heard every excuse in the book.

When you get your first letter from the collection agency, it must state the amount of the debt and the name of the original creditor along with the information that you have 30 days to dispute the validity of the debt and that if you do dispute it, the agency will send you verification from the creditor of the debt owed.

It is a good idea to request verification of the debt in any case. There could be charges that you do not agree with and can dispute, thus delaying any further collection activity for several weeks or even months. This would give you additional time to raise the money to pay off the debt.

When the collection agency telephones you, stay calm. The call will be anything but pleasant if you can't pay the bill. A typical conversation from a collection agency would be as follows:

*Collector:* Hello, Mrs. B. My name is Kelly from ABC Collections. You have an outstanding balance owed to Arlington Department Store for $652. We need to receive $652 by next week. When will you be sending it?

*Debtor:* I'm sorry, but we don't have the money. My husband was laid off his job and I can't pay it at the present time.

*Collector:* I understand your situation, Mrs. B; however, you do owe the money and we have been instructed to collect. What can you send?

*Debtor:* Nothing at this time.

*Collector:* Mrs. B, surely you understand that our client could sue you to collect this bill.

*Debtor:* I don't have the money now to pay you.

*Collector:* Mrs. B, you will be hearing from us again!

When you're talking to a collector, be sure you know what you can afford to pay. Collectors initially will try to collect the entire amount you owe, but after several unsuccessful attempts, they will usually settle for something less. Don't let them pressure you into paying anything if you need the money for essential living expenses, such as housing, food, and utilities. Review your list of essentials.

Collection agencies are hard to brush off. They will write letters or make frequent telephone calls. They know that if they can reach you within the first three months after your account became delinquent, they will have a higher success rate in collecting. The older the debt, the harder it is for them to collect.

Communicate with the collection agency when you have something to say. If you can set up a repayment plan for the account, do it. If you can't, then talk to the agency occasionally to explain your situation. But don't offer more information than you need to. Be vague in your answers. Stick to what you can or cannot do.

## Negotiating with the Collection Agency

Collection agencies, as I've mentioned, must follow the instructions of the original creditor, and any negotiating must be approved by that creditor. The collection agency has specific instructions about what it can negotiate, and any divergence from the original instructions must be approved.

Before you start negotiating with the collector, prepare a definite plan. Review your debt list for items you can pay.

If you decide to offer a lump sum to settle the debt, remember that each collection agency has a different policy. Some will take 60 to 80 percent of the debt; others may take 50 percent. Know your bottom line. If you have a bill for $700 and know you can pay $400, offer $400. Remember, no matter what you offer, the agency will try to get more. If $400 is all you can pay, then stick to that amount. Tell the collector that $400 is your final offer and you want him to take the $400 as payment in full and remove the debt from your credit report. If the collector agrees, get a statement in writing from the agency indicating that upon receipt of the agreed amount, it will accept that amount as payment in full and will remove the debt from all your credit reports. It is important to get the agreement in writing from the collection agency before you send in a payment.

As soon as you receive the letter, follow through immediately with the payment in full. If you have several accounts in collection, offer whatever lump sums you have to settle them.

Many times a collection agency employee will say to you, "We can discount your balance by 20 percent if you pay it off immediately." Most people aren't able to do that, and so they refuse the offer. The agency representative would then say, "If you can only pay a lesser amount, then the discount will not apply, and the total balance is owed."

If you offer monthly payments, the collection agency has little motivation to agree to anything less than the total balance. It still will have to follow through to collect. Many times after one or two payments, you'll stop paying and the agency will have to resume collection efforts. If you offer monthly payments, do follow through until the debt is paid off. Before you make your final payment, contact the agency and ask for a letter stating that upon receipt of the final payment, the agency will remove the entry from your credit report.

### *Things to Remember When Negotiating*

1. Whenever you talk to a collector, let him or her know all the financial problems you have: a job layoff, back taxes, illnesses, or whatever.

2. If you're considering filing for bankruptcy, let the collector know. Many times the collector will try to talk you out of it.

3. Don't give the agency any information about your place of business or bank.

4. Pay the collection agency with a money order from a bank where you have no accounts or from the post office.

5. Periodically communicate with the collection agency. Failure to communicate with the agency may expedite further collection action such as a lawsuit.

6. If you hire a lawyer to negotiate with the creditor, make sure the debt is large enough to make it worth your while. If a lawyer charges $150 an hour and your bill is only $500, it would be foolish to pay both the bill and the lawyer. If your debt is several thousand dollars and you may be able to get a substantial reduction, then it's worth engaging a lawyer.

7. If you bought an item that was used as security for the debt, offer to return it to the collection agency. If the agency or original creditor agrees to take the item back, have the agency write a letter stating that the item itself is payment in full and that a deficiency judgment will not be filed. If the agency refuses, then try to sell the item to raise the money for repaying the debt.

8. Never lose your composure or your temper when negotiating. Stay in control of the situation. Know your plan beforehand. If you cannot repay the debt, explain that you will inform the agency when you are able to make some sort of payment.

## How Collection Agencies Find You

Collection agencies have several ways of tracking you down when they're trying to collect a debt. When a collection agency calls or writes you, the agency does not necessarily know where you live. The only thing it knows is that the bill it sent you was not returned. Several ways collection agencies use to locate you and ways to avoid being found are discussed below.

**Credit application information.** The most logical way to find you is through a credit application. The original creditor will supply the collection agency with information from your initial application: your full name, address, telephone number, Social Security number, employer, bank, credit references, and nearest living relative. Even if you've moved, someone listed on your credit application would undoubtedly know how to locate you.

If you do move, don't disclose your new address except to a few people you can trust.

**Post office.** A collection agency may check the post office for your forwarding address, so don't leave a forwarding address if you do not wish to be found. Give your new address only to companies and individuals that you will have contact with on a regular basis.

**Employers.** A collection agency may call your employer while posing as a long-lost friend or relative. Instruct your employer not to give your address to anyone.

**Neighbors.** A collection agency may use a cross (or street) directory that is published by the telephone company and matches phone numbers to addresses. If your telephone number is unlisted, however, it will not appear, but a cross directory does provide the names and phone numbers of people living in your neighborhood.

**Department of motor vehicles.** In most states, a collection agency can get such information as your name and address for a minimal fee payable to the state's department of motor vehicles. The information appears when you reregister your car.

**Voter registration.** Some collection agencies may check voter registration records in the county where you reside. If you've moved and reregistered in the same county, your new address will appear.

**Banks.** If you have moved but kept your same bank account, a collection agency may try to get your new address from the bank. It's better if you close your bank account and reopen one at a different bank.

**Credit bureaus.** Some collection agencies are associated with credit bureaus. In such cases, the agency has access to all your credit history. Even if the collection agency is not associated with a credit bureau, for a small fee it can be placed on a list to locate you. Sometimes entries on a credit report say "SCNL," which means the credit grantor cannot locate the individual. Because of the fee paid to the credit bureau, anytime you try to get credit and a credit report is run, the credit bureau will forward your name to the collection agency, even if you have moved out of state.

Do not apply for any new credit while you have ongoing debt problems.

## Filing a Complaint against a Collection Agency

If you feel at any time that a collection agency has violated the Fair Debt Collection Practices Act, you can file a complaint with the Federal Trade Commission, your state attorney general's office, or any other office that regulates collection agencies.

The law is very specific about what a collection agency can or cannot do.

### The Best Solution

The best solution when dealing with a collection agency is to pay your bill as quickly as possible. Consumer laws are intended to provide a chance for you to work out your problems without harassment.

Try to pay the creditor directly rather than the collection agency. If the creditor accepts the payment, let the collection agency know the bill was paid. Make sure the creditor and the agency remove any negative item on your credit report. If the creditor will not accept the payment, pay the bill as soon as possible to the collection agency.

The federal law, as already indicated, applies to collection agencies, but some creditors have their own collection departments or lawyers to whom the federal rules do not apply.

If you feel you are being unjustly harassed, seek the advice of an attorney.

## Some Final Words

1. If a collection agency calls, indicate that you know your rights and that you wish to know the name and address of the collector. Be sure to write it down. Remain calm and polite during the conversation. Try to resolve the problem and make the necessary arrangements.

2. If no solution is reached and you feel you've said all that need be said and you don't wish any further discussion with, or correspondence from, the collection agency, write a letter to the agency expressing your wish for no further discussion or communication. Send it certified mail with a return receipt. Be prepared for one final response telling you what the collection agency proposes to do and naming a possible court date. The agency, on the other hand, may possibly write you off as a bad debt.

3. If you have questions or disputes about a bill, be sure to write a letter to the collection agency within 30 days of receiving the bill. The agency must verify the bill and during the time it is doing so, it cannot try to collect the bill. Send the letter certified mail with a return receipt. Be sure to keep all copies of correspondence.

4. If you have a major complaint about the collection agency and feel your rights have been violated, file a formal complaint with the Federal Trade Commission and your state attorney general.

## Collection Agency Worksheet

Use this worksheet to keep records of all telephone calls and letters from a collection agency.

Collection agency name: _____

Original creditor: _____

Date of first notice: _____

Date you sent verification: _____


Notes on telephone communication: _____

Date: _____

Person you spoke with: _____

Conversation: _____

_____

_____

_____


Date: _____

Person you spoke with: _____

Conversation: _____

_____

_____

_____

# Chapter 8

# Free at Last!
## Getting Out of Debt

## Raising Cash and Getting Out of Debt

There are ways to reduce your debt as well as pay off your debt. The following suggestions may help you decrease your credit load.

### Major Credit Cards

If you have major credit cards that are not delinquent or charged to the maximum credit limit, move your high-interest credit card balances to your credit cards with a low interest rate. Review the interest rates and annual fees you're charged for the use of all your credit cards. For example, you have two credit cards. One has a credit limit of $2,000, an interest rate of 16 percent, and a balance of $500. Your other credit card has a credit limit of $2,500, an interest rate of 19 percent, and a balance of $1,000. Get a cash advance from your credit card with the 16 percent interest rate and pay off the credit card with the $1,000 balance. You would now owe $1,500 on the card with the 16 percent interest rate. You are saving 3 percent interest. Add the payment you would be making on the card with the 19 percent interest rate to the payment you would make on the credit card with the 16 percent interest rate. Your balance will come down rapidly and save you money in interest charges.

## Major Assets

If you need to raise money in a hurry, you can sell a major asset—a home, a car, furniture, jewelry, computer equipment, and so on. Anything of substantial value can be sold to raise money for relieving a large debt.

If you have a loan for a major asset, sell the asset to pay off the loan. For example, if you sold your house for $200,000 and had a first mortgage of $120,000 and a second mortgage of $25,000 with $16,000 in closing costs, your net profit would be $39,000. You could use the $39,000 to pay off your debts and help you relocate to a new residence.

If you have assets on which you do not owe money, you can use the money you receive from the sale of those assets to apply toward your debt. Look around at what assets you may have. Are they things you can live without and are not using? If you don't need it, sell the asset (refer to the Marketable Assets Worksheet).

## Home Equity Loans and Refinancing

A home equity loan, known as a second mortgage, or a refinancing of your first mortgage can benefit you if you don't want to sell your property.

When you refinance your property or try to obtain a second mortgage, you must have enough equity in the property for a lender to approve the loan. The lender will usually lend 60 to 90 percent of the appraised value of your property minus the amount you still owe on it. For example, if your house is worth $200,000 and you still owe $120,000 on it, the lender would loan you $40,000. You calculate like this: 80 percent of $200,000 is $160,000; subtract $120,000 from $160,000, which equals $40,000. After subtracting loan fees and costs from the $40,000, the amount remaining is your net cash.

There are 100 percent and 125 percent equity loans, too, but they are harder to qualify for; however, you can be prequalified by a lender. Professional Credit Counselors will review your current situation and help you get the loan you need. Call or write Professional Credit Counselors, 1100 Irvine Blvd., #541, Tustin, CA 92780; 714-541-2637.

If you decide to refinance your house or take out a second mortgage, you need to make sure your payments will be reduced after you pay off your debts. If they are not, don't refinance. Remember that you

## Marketable Assets Worksheet

Make a list of the assets you can sell to raise cash, which could include your home, a car, jewelry, furniture, or electronic equipment—anything of value that you can live without.

Asset                                                                 Amount

_____

_____

_____

_____

_____

_____

_____

_____

_____

_____

_____

_____

_____

_____

_____

                                                                      Total

are already having problems paying what you owe without increasing your debt or payments.

Refinancing or taking out a second mortgage requires many more years to pay off the mortgage. Ask yourself, "Will my bills (excluding my mortgage) be paid off within three years if I keep my present mortgage?" If the answer is yes, reconsider refinancing. You will have to pay loan fees and the new mortgage could be for 15 to 30 years, depending on the type of loan. Do you want to be strapped with the new payment for that long?

### Mortgage Reduction Plan

There is a way to reduce the life of your mortgage, which usually is for 30 years, by setting yourself up on a mortgage reduction plan. By adding additional money to your house payment each month, you can save possibly hundreds of thousands of dollars for the life of your loan and have a 30-year loan paid off several years early, perhaps even as early as 15 years.

By adding one extra payment a year, you can cut the life of a 30-year loan by approximately 15 to 17 years.

## Friends or Family

During a financial crisis, friends or family will often lend you money, which is only beneficial if they are flexible in being paid back. If you are close to filing for bankruptcy and a friend or relative loans you money to make payments that will be discharged in the bankruptcy, use the loan for an essential need rather than for one that will be discharged.

## Debt Consolidation Companies

Debt consolidation companies can be helpful if you choose the right company. A few companies will actually invest their funds to bring past due payments up to date. To preserve or enhance your credit, choose a company that invests its own money to help you get back on track.

When you contract with that type of debt consolidation company, the company will rapidly bring your accounts current by combining your payments and using its own funds. The term of the contract is determined at the outset, giving you a target date to be completely debt free and giving you the ability to set up a convenient, level payment program that will remain fixed until the end of your contract.

Credi-Care can offer you a personalized debt consolidation program to fit your needs. You can contact them by writing Credi-Care, Inc., Dept. 703, P.O. Box 13007, Birmingham, AL 35202-3007; or telephone them at 800-LAST-BIL, ext. #703.

## Extra Credit Card Payments

By adding an extra payment, even $5 or $10 to your monthly credit card payment, your debt will be paid off more quickly and you'll save a large amount in interest charges. Look at the sample chart below and see the difference in savings:

## Sample Credit Card Chart

If you were to pay $5 or $10 extra toward your payment each month, look at the savings.

| Balance | # of Months Until Paid | Total Interest Paid | $5 Extra Interest Saved | Saved # of Months | $10 Extra Interest Saved | Saved # of Months |
|---|---|---|---|---|---|---|
| $2,000 | 193 | $2,504.62 | $738.59 | 70 | $1,113.70 | 101 |
| 1,900 | 189 | 2,364.62 | 714.91 | 69 | 1,073.24 | 100 |
| 1,800 | 185 | 2,224.65 | 690.21 | 69 | 1,031.26 | 99 |
| 1,700 | 180 | 2,084.61 | 664.31 | 67 | 987.56 | 97 |
| 1,600 | 176 | 1,944.63 | 637.15 | 67 | 942.14 | 96 |
| 1,500 | 171 | 1,804.61 | 608.60 | 66 | 894.78 | 94 |
| 1,400 | 165 | 1,664.65 | 578.54 | 65 | 845.32 | 92 |
| 1,300 | 159 | 1,524.64 | 546.71 | 63 | 793.55 | 90 |
| 1,200 | 153 | 1,384.64 | 512.96 | 62 | 739.26 | 87 |
| 1,100 | 146 | 1,244.65 | 477.06 | 60 | 682.17 | 85 |
| 1,000 | 138 | 1,104.63 | 438.66 | 58 | 621.95 | 81 |

## Tax Refund

Getting a tax refund can be a hidden miracle if done quickly. If you're facing a financial crisis but have a tax refund due, there are ways you can get your refund without waiting the usual time.

Contact the IRS directly. Every IRS office has a Problem Resolution Program, which has been set up to assist taxpayers. To contact your local office, check the government listings in your telephone book for the Problem Resolution Program (PRP) department of the federal Internal Revenue Service.

Some finance companies and tax preparation services offer quick tax refunds, so you can check your telephone directory for the one nearest you.

## Refinancing an Automobile

Refinancing an automobile can bring you cash and, in most instances, lower your monthly payment. Remember, however, that you are prolonging the life of the loan by refinancing, thus paying more interest.

When you refinance your car, the bank or other lender takes the blue book (a periodically issued price list) value and subtracts the amount that you owe. The difference between the loan amount and the amount you owe is the amount of cash you would receive. For example, if the blue book value was $5,000 and you have a balance due of $3,000, the $2,000 difference would be your equity or cash due you.

If you have to refinance your car, try to pay additional money with each payment to shorten the life of the loan. Write on your payment coupon, "Apply the difference of this payment toward my principal." The car will be paid back much more quickly and your interest payments reduced.

## Pawnshop

A pawnshop should be your last resort when trying to raise quick cash. At a pawnshop you leave your property in return for a loan from the pawnbroker. Many people pawn jewelry, electronic equipment, photography equipment, antiques, musical instruments, firearms, golf clubs, and similar items. A pawnbroker will usually take anything that has resale value.

The problem with using a pawnshop is that you will only receive approximately 50 to 60 percent of an item's resale value, and brokers charge a high interest rate. You are usually allowed a few months to repay the loan, but if you don't repay when the loan is due, the property you left becomes the property of the pawnshop and the pawnbroker then will probably sell the item.

In some states you are entitled to the money collected over and above what you owe if a pawnbroker sells your property and receives more for it than what you owe on the loan plus storage fees and sales costs.

Don't use a pawnshop if you have no way of repaying the pawnbroker's loan. Once your property is sold, you have no way to retrieve it.

## Part-Time Job

Getting a part-time job is another way of earning additional cash. Before you do, analyze the number of hours you are working now to see if you can put in more time on your current full-time job. The job you have may offer overtime hours. If not, check the classified section of your local newspaper under employment opportunities for jobs requiring two to four hours a day. If any fit your schedule, follow up on the ads.

---

## ✎ Money-Making Hobbies Worksheet

Make a list of the hobbies or talents you have that could earn money.

_____

_____

_____

_____

_____

_____

_____

_____

_____

_____

_____

_____

_____

_____

_____

_____

_____

_____

---

Make sure, however, that you will come out ahead without spending excess money in travel time, clothing, child care, and food. The key is to make enough extra money so you can pay off your bills.

The jobs that are offered may require special skills. If that is the case, brush up on your specialty or go back to school to update your skills so you have the opportunity to make more money in the long run.

### Hobby

Use your hobby to make money. You may be proficient in mechanical areas, crafts, electronics, photography, carpentry, or cooking. Analyze what special talents you possess. Advertise what you can do and make a profit from doing the things you enjoy (fill in the Money-Making Hobbies Worksheet).

Everybody is gifted and has different talents. There is a job for everybody. You may be good in repairing cars, whereas another individual could never do such a thing. Others may understand electronics, whereas you could never imagine yourself working with electronics. See if you can fill a need to help others and make money at the same time.

## Bartering

Bartering may not get you cash, but it also will not get you into debt. When economic conditions are tough, many businesses will barter—that is, they will accept from you a service or item that has value in exchange for a service. You may have something they want and they may have something you want. Make an offer. It may save you money.

## Bankruptcy

Is bankruptcy for you? Too often a debtor will take the easy way out by filing for bankruptcy without thinking of the possible consequences. Financial problems have a way of tormenting a person day and night. It causes such mental distress that bankruptcy seems the easy way out.

There are three types of bankruptcies: Chapter 7 pertains to everyone and Chapter 13 pertains to individuals; Chapter 11 pertains to a business reorganization and also to individuals. Individuals can only qualify for a Chapter 11 if their debt is larger than the maximum debt a Chapter 13 allows or they are a business. Our discussion focuses on Chapter 7 and Chapter 13 bankruptcies.

## Chapter 7 Bankruptcy

A Chapter 7, known as a straight bankruptcy, is a debtor's most powerful tool. It is a way to make most debts disappear without having to repay them. It results in a fresh clean start and freedom from the burden of past debts. It sounds like an easy solution, but many times a debtor is misadvised and pressured into filing for bankruptcy.

When filing for bankruptcy, you can get the necessary forms from your local stationery store in whatever state you reside. To find the nearest courthouse, look in the telephone book under United States Bankruptcy Court. Call the bankruptcy clerk to find out which court is the correct one for your county and district. Find out from the clerk how long you must have been a resident in that county before you are eligible to file. All states require 91 days residency before you can file (the law actually requires the greater part of the past 180 days, so the 91 days do not have to be consecutive). You are allowed to keep some property, so you must know what the laws are in your state for exempting property.

The forms you file are very lengthy but must be filled out. Basically, they ask for a list of all your debts and all your property. The day you return your forms and pay the filing fee to the bankruptcy clerk, you may stop paying your debts. Notify creditors immediately by phone followed up by writing if you want them to stop collecting from you.

## Trustee

Approximately one month after you file the bankruptcy papers, you must go to a meeting with the trustee, that is, the person in charge of your bankruptcy. It is the bankruptcy trustee's job to determine if you have any nonexempt property which must be turned over to the trustee. During the meeting, the trustee will ask questions to determine which items, if any, of your property can be taken.

A couple of months after the initial meeting, a discharge, meaning a formal forgiveness of your debts, will be granted. The likelihood of getting rid of *all* your debts is unrealistic.

A dischargeable debt disappears after bankruptcy, so you are legally free not to pay that debt. Most unsecured debts in fact after bankruptcy are dischargeable; they include credit card purchases, medical bills, and rent.

A nondischargeable debt is not affected by bankruptcy, and thus you must repay it. Examples of nondischargeable debts include certain taxes, alimony, and some student loans.

## Unsecured Debt

A debt is unsecured if you never signed a written agreement pledging some of your property as potential payment of the debt. Examples of unsecured debts are most credit card and charge purchases, and personal loans from friends or relatives.

## Secured Debt

A secured debt is created when you make a written promise that the creditor can take a particular item of your property if you do not pay. The item may be what you purchased but not necessarily. Examples of secured debts include motor vehicles, expensive jewelry, and furniture. Most secured debts are dischargeable in bankruptcy if you return the collateral; however, you can keep the property if you make payments and have the account reaffirmed by the court.

Bankruptcy is a serious matter and one that should be thought out and researched. Most libraries have several good books that can help you understand the process in greater detail. There are do-it-yourself bankruptcy books, but make sure you understand state and federal laws regulating the bankruptcy process. Contact an attorney who specializes in bankruptcy for answers to questions you probably will still have.

## Your Credit Report

Many people believe their credit reports will be wiped clean when they file for bankruptcy. That is wrong. The bankruptcy will appear on the credit report as a public notice. All of your creditors that report to a particular credit reporting agency will appear in the negative column, which can further hurt your chances of obtaining new credit. Bankruptcies are reported on your credit report for up to ten years.

## Stopping Harassment by Creditors

Many attorneys advertise: "Stop creditors' harassment." In essence, they are suggesting bankruptcy.

A Chapter 13 is known as the federal repayment plan or wage earners plan and is a way of avoiding a Chapter 7 straight bankruptcy. The basic concept of a Chapter 13 is to provide court supervision and protection so debtors can develop and perform a plan to repay their debts in whole or in part over a three- to five-year period. The plan is a budget you learn to live with until it is paid.

Filing a Chapter 13 repayment plan is better than a consolidation loan because you pay no interest or finance charges on most debts. You can determine the amount of your monthly payments and decide how much of your debts you are able to pay.

Filling out and filing forms for a Chapter 13 stops all creditor harassment and collection efforts. You can also stop wage garnishments but only if creditors are notified immediately (in writing). All payments thereafter are made through a court-appointed trustee according to your repayment terms.

Approximately one month after you file your forms, you must meet with the trustee. The trustee will want to go over the budget you designed to make sure it will succeed. In most districts debtors do not attend the confirmation hearing; usually only the trustee and the debtor's attorney attend. The creditors too must agree to go along with the plan. If the creditors agree and the judge finds that your plan complies with the law, he or she will confirm it, and it will go into immediate operation. It could be several months after the creditors' meeting, however, before your plan is confirmed.

Most repayment plans call for payments on all or almost all of your debts over a three-year period; some may be as long as five years. During that time you will repay the trustee a certain amount each month and the trustee will take care of all your bills and deal with your creditors. If you have kept your agreement at the end of your repayment period, the court forgives any remaining balance due on all the debts covered by your plan.

The main difference between a straight bankruptcy and a Chapter 13 is that a straight bankruptcy (a Chapter 7) wipes out most debts without their being repaid. A straight bankruptcy is often a good idea for those who cannot realistically expect to pay a significant portion of their debts within a reasonable time. A Chapter 13 is good for those whose financial problems are not as severe. It provides a way for you to repay your debts over a certain time period under court supervision and protection. It also helps you keep secured items like cars or furniture by lowering the payments.

A Chapter 13 will appear on your credit report where it will remain up to ten years. Because a payment program has been established, it is up to each creditor to decide what to report.

Making a decision of whether to file for bankruptcy should be considered carefully. Make an appointment with an attorney to learn about all your options.

## Chapter 13 versus Consumer Credit Counseling

Many creditors will cooperate with you if you are working with Consumer Credit Counseling Service (CCCS), and then you may not want to file a Chapter 13. Either way, you'd still have a repayment program by which you would be giving money monthly to a third party, who in turn would pay your creditors. Reports to the credit reporting bureaus are made under both programs; a bankruptcy notation, however, is usually considered worse than a notation that you are working with CCCS. Fees are assessed for filing a Chapter 13 bankruptcy, and a monthly fee is charged by CCCS.

There are two main differences between filing a Chapter 13 and working with CCCS. First, if you miss a payment to a creditor during your bankruptcy court repayment program, creditors are barred under Chapter 13 from initiating any collection procedures. CCCS, on the other hand, cannot offer any protection to you against any collection activity.

Second, when repaying your debt under Chapter 13, you are usually paying less than you actually owe. At the end of the three- to five-year period, you are not required to pay off any outstanding balances. The bankruptcy rating on your credit report indicates that the creditors have been paid. If your home is threatened with an imminent foreclosure, you can stop the foreclosure under a Chapter 13 and have payments stretched out up to five years.

CCCS's repayment plan, on the other hand, requires the total amount owed to be repaid in full; CCCS in fact is paid by the creditors. A negative credit entry may be made on your credit report if you are paying less than the amount required. Your account will thus continue to show late payments, which in turn has a negative impact on your credit report.

# Chapter 9

## You Can Run but You Can't Hide!

### The Price You Pay for Ignoring Your Debts

Ignoring your bills will not make them go away. Too often we think, If I close my eyes, and pretend they do not exist, my bills will disappear. Unfortunately, that is not how it works: bills rarely go away. If your balance is small enough, a creditor may write it off, but don't count on it. If you ignore your bills long enough, your creditors may take legal action to collect.

## Possible Consequences of Ignoring Your Bills

**Eviction.** When you fall behind in your rent, your landlord may evict you from your residence. The landlord must first give you notice, but if you refuse to move, you would probably be served with a subpoena to appear in court on a certain date. You then have a certain number of days to respond.

If you do not respond and ignore the lawsuit, the landlord can have an automatic judgment entered against you. The judgment goes to the local sheriff's office, and you are notified by the sheriff at least one week in advance of the eviction date to move. If you don't move by that date, the sheriff will enforce the eviction.

**Foreclosure.**  When you fall behind in making your mortgage pay-ments, very rarely does the lender rush out and initiate a foreclosure. If several payments have been missed, however, the lender has a right to foreclose on your home and probably will.

The entire foreclosure process can take 9 to 18 months to com-plete. If you are living in the home during that time, you are living there rent free, so start saving your money to relocate or catch up on your back payments.

Once you have missed a payment, you will begin receiving a series of letters requesting payment; you'll receive telephone calls as well. After several months of calls and letters to no avail, the lender will file a notice of default and send it to you by certified mail. A notice of default states that foreclosure proceedings have begun and it is usually reported on your credit report.

Once you have received a default notice, you have approximately 90 days to bring the account current. (Check with your state; each state is different.) You have to pay all the past due payments plus late fees and other charges.

If you do not bring the account current at the end of 90 days, the lender sets a date for a public sale of your property, which usually occurs approximately 30 days from the date of the first publishing. The published notice lists the address of the house, information about the loan, and the time and location of the sale. Some lenders will let you rein-state the loan before the sale; others may require a total payoff of the loan balance. Each state has its own policies.

At the foreclosure sale, anyone can bid on the property. The lender who has foreclosed on your property (usually the holder of the first deed of trust) makes the first bid. The first bid is the amount owed the lender. If there is a second and/or third deed of trust on the property, the holders will probably be in attendance. Other creditors who have an interest in the property also will be there and can bid on the property to protect their interest. If nobody bids above the foreclosing lender's bid, the property goes back to the lender for the amount of its bid.

In some cases, the property may be sold for less than the amount owed, which could result in a deficiency judgment. Not all states honor a deficiency in a foreclosure sale, so it is important that you know what your state's regulations are if you are faced with a foreclosure.

You can avoid a foreclosure by selling your house or offering the property back to the lender by means of a quitclaim deed.

**Repossession.** As previously explained, a secured debt is one that has collateral guaranteeing an item for repayment, so the lender can take the item you have guaranteed for the loan if you don't repay.

The most common types of loans involving collateral are for the following:

- Motor vehicles—cars, boats, trucks, vans, RVs, and the like
- Furniture, electronic equipment, and major appliances
- Personal items such as cars, jewelry, and furniture

If you miss a payment on a secured loan, the lender could repossess the item. It only takes one missed payment for repossession; however, if you stay in touch with the lender and pay the amount due within a reasonable time, the lender will usually not rush in to repossess the item. If the lender feels insecure in any way, however, it does have the option to repossess the item at any time.

If you have an item repossessed—for example, your car—you usually will have 60 to 90 days to reinstate the loan. If you don't reinstate it during that period, the lender can then sell the item.

Be sure to read your security agreement thoroughly before you secure any item. If it looks as though you may have problems making your payments, sell the item to avoid a repossession. If you don't, you may face a deficiency judgment if the lender ends up selling the item; and you'll still owe the lender money.

**Deficiency judgment.** If you have an item that is repossessed and you do not reinstate the item, the lender can sell the item to raise cash for paying at least some of the debt.

When the lender has a date for the sale, you must be notified. The sale can be one of two kinds. It is either a public sale, which is open to anyone, or a private sale to which the lender invites only interested prospects. If the sale is open to the public, you must be notified of the date, time, and location; if it is a private sale, you may be told only the date.

If you have a car, for example, worth $11,000 on which you owe $8,000, and it is sold at a repossession sale for $5,000, there is a deficiency, or difference, of $3,000 that you owe the lender. The lender will also add to the deficiency the cost of repossessing, storing, and selling the item.

In other words, the balance you owe after the repossession sale is the deficiency. A lender will immediately start trying to collect the balance; if you refuse to pay, the lender can go to court to obtain a deficiency judgment against you for the payment.

The deficiency is reported on your credit report; the repossession is listed as well as the amount owed. Thus, it is always better to try to sell the secured item yourself. If you can do this before it is repossessed, you can pay off the debt and perhaps have enough money left over to pay other bills.

If you are in a difficult financial situation and you intend to file for bankruptcy, the deficiency judgment will probably be discharged by the court.

**Lawsuit.**  If you do not pay your debt, more than likely the creditor will sue you. If the amount owed is relatively little, the creditor may give up trying to collect. If the creditor feels you are in a judgment-proof situation—that is, you have no money, property, or assets now and probably won't in the near future—the creditor may not follow through with a lawsuit.

A creditor that seeks a remedy through small claims court is able to obtain a judgment much quicker than by going through the regular court system. If you do not appear to defend yourself in small claims court, you will automatically lose the suit and a judgment against you entered.

If you fight a suit in a regular court, it may take several years. If you contest the lawsuit, you must respond to the initial court papers you are served within the time period provided by the laws of your state. If you do not respond, you will automatically lose.

If the creditor does obtain a judgment against you, there are a number of ways the judgment can be enforced. In some states, one way is to attach your wages if you are employed—but only a portion of your paycheck may be taken until the debt is paid.

Once a judgment is entered against you, the court sends it to the county recorders office, where it becomes a public notice. The credit reporting bureaus receive their information from the county recorder's office and note the judgment on your credit report. When the judgment is paid off, the court notifies the county recorder's office, which again documents the order. Listed on the credit report will be the name of the creditor, the amount owed, and the date of the judgment. Having a judgment on your report hurts your chances of getting new credit until the debt is paid. If you are trying to buy a house, the debt must be paid off before completion of the sale.

If you are considering bankruptcy and have a judgment against you, the judgment probably will be discharged by the court, which means you don't have to pay it.

**Liens on real property.** A common method a creditor uses to collect what you owe is to obtain a court judgment placing a lien on your property.

When you sell your house or other property, you must have a clear title; but with a lien, the title is not clear. Thus, a sale cannot be completed until the lien is removed, which usually occurs before the completion, or at the close, of your escrow. Placing a lien on your property is an almost sure way for a creditor to eventually collect what you owe.

Other types of liens include the following:

- State or property taxes owed
- Internal Revenue taxes owed
- Child support or alimony owed
- Money owed to a contractor who has done work for you

# Part Three

# Credit Restoration/ Credit Repair

# Chapter 10

# Credit Facelift!
## Restoring Your Credit

Thousands of people are turned down for credit each day because of negative, but inaccurate, entries on their credit reports.

Credit cards and good credit ratings are a must in today's society. Too often a credit report is damaged as a result of hospitalization, illness, divorce, or unemployment. If you have had a setback and your bills have fallen behind, your creditors will probably report your payment pattern, good or bad, to at least one credit reporting agency.

This chapter on credit restoration is designed to assist you in improving your credit reports by challenging inaccurate information and to help you rebuild your credit reports by establishing new credit.

## Current Credit Problems: A Warning

If you have credit problems and outstanding bills now, this chapter is not for you. Your credit problems should be at least one year old before you work on your credit report. The more time that has elapsed, the better the chances of removing or correcting information on your credit report. As you read through this chapter, you will gain a new understanding of the procedures used to repair and enhance your credit reports.

If your bills are still outstanding, pay them before you try to repair an inaccurate credit report. But if an item entered on your credit report is 100 percent accurate, don't dispute it.

Credit repair companies can assist you with your problem credit reports. Whereas they charge a large fee for their services, the information offered in this book is the same as a credit repair company offers. But no one can guarantee removal or correction of any one item on a credit report. Save yourself some money and do it yourself. If you need to consult a credit consultant, contact Professional Credit Counselors, 1100 Irvine Blvd., #541, Tustin, CA 92780; 714-541-2637.

## Introduction to Credit Restoration

If your credit application has been turned down, the creditor must send you a letter within 30 days indicating the reason and which reporting agency was used to obtain credit information on you.

Whenever an application is turned down, you are entitled to a free credit report from the credit reporting agency listed in the denial letter. The credit report must be requested within 60 days of the denial letter. A copy of the denial letter should be included with your request or at least mentioned in your letter to the credit reporting agency. (See Sample Credit Report Request Form 1B for rejected applicants.)

### Get Updates

It is a good idea to have an updated report on yourself from all the major credit reporting agencies that report in your state. It may be Experian (formerly TRW), Trans Union, or Equifax. If you aren't sure which agencies are dominant in your community, you can find out from a bank or mortgage company. There may be only one or two in your area; every city and state is different. If you haven't been turned down for credit, the credit reporting agency charges a fee for the report. Each state has its own fee, so call the credit reporting office to find out what its fee is. Remember that a husband and wife don't have a combined report; each has an individual report even with joint accounts. And you must send the fee for each report.

## Sample Credit Request Form—Form #1A

SAMPLE ONLY! DO NOT USE!!

Dear Credit Bureau,

Please send me a copy of my credit report. I am enclosing the necessary fee.

Name _____

Current Address _____

City _____ State _____ Zip _____

Previous Address _____

City _____ State _____ Zip _____

Social Security # _____

Year of Birth _____

Sincerely,

(Sign name)

MAIL THIS TYPE OF LETTER IF YOU HAVE NOT BEEN TURNED DOWN FOR CREDIT. SEND TO: EXPERIAN, TRANS UNION, and EQUIFAX.

Also enclose a copy of your drivers license and any bill with your name and address printed on it for identification.

After obtaining a copy or copies of your credit report, review each entry. Each report has a breakdown of all the codes accompanying the reports; you can also review the code breakdown presented in Chapter 3. If you find any items on your report that you feel are inaccurate, incorrect, erroneous, or incomplete, you have a right to dispute them. The Fair Credit Reporting Act provides that any dispute over a consumer credit report must be reinvestigated and removed if found to be inaccurate and/or unverifiable or if the creditor does not respond.

The credit reporting agency will complete its investigation within 30 days of receiving a letter describing your dispute. If the creditor does

## Sample Credit Request Form—Form #1B

SAMPLE ONLY! DO NOT USE!!

Dear Credit Bureau,

Please send me a copy of my credit report. I was turned down for credit by
_____ (insert name of company).

Name _____

Current Address _____

City _____ State _____ Zip _____

Previous Address _____

City _____ State _____ Zip _____

Social Security # _____

Year of Birth _____

Sincerely,

(Sign name)

MAIL THIS TYPE OF LETTER IF YOU WERE TURNED DOWN FOR CREDIT.
NO FEE IS NECESSARY. SEND TO: EXPERIAN, TRANS UNION, and EQUIFAX.

Also enclose a copy of your drivers license and any bill with your name and
address printed on it for identification.

not respond, the credit reporting agency must remove the negative
entry from the report. If the creditor does respond and the item is not
removed, you can write a 100-word statement on any of the remaining
items on the credit report explaining why the problem occurred. It then
will be on the report every time a credit report is run. If you don't want
to write a statement on the report, wait approximately 120 days after
receiving the updated credit report and try disputing the item again.
Repeat the procedure as necessary. Remember that the credit reporting

agency must dispute the item with the creditor unless the agency feels it is irrelevant or frivolous.

You may feel more comfortable letting a credit consulting company assist you. You are capable of handling it yourself, but a fee is charged if you use a consulting company. Make sure the company you select is reputable.

## Step-by-Step Guide to Credit Repair

**Step 1:** Copy the appropriate Sample Credit Request Form to request a current copy of your credit report from the credit reporting agency in your area: Experian, Trans Union, and Equifax. If you have applied for credit within the past 60 days and been turned down, the credit agency charges no fee. If you have not applied for credit recently, you must enclose a fee. Each state has different fees. Call the bureau to find out the amount for your state.

When requesting a credit report, most people incorrectly assume that a husband and wife are considered as one. The majority of credit, both good and bad, usually shows up on the husband's file, but the wife's file probably has good and bad entries also. If either spouse ever wants to apply for credit separately, it's a good idea to have the report cleared of all inaccurate negative items.

**Step 2:** Approximately two weeks after the requests for your credit reports have been sent, you will receive the updated reports. Analyze all the items being reported. There will be a key to help you in determining the negative items. Look to see if the accounts are being accurately reported. For example, check account numbers, status of the accounts, amounts owed, dates, and anything else that looks incorrect. Use the sample responses form for the possible excuse you may have or one you feel is appropriate.

Write a letter to each of the three major credit reporting agencies for each inaccurate entry. Do not dispute more than four to six entries on one letter or form. Mail one letter every 30 days until all the items you are disputing are reported. Send the letters by regular mail. The dates are important. Keep copies of all the letters you send. (See Sample Dispute Letter Forms 2A and 2B. *Notice the dates* in our sample letters.)

## Sample Dispute Letter—Form #2A

June 19, 1996

Dear Credit Bureau,

After receiving a copy of my credit report, I have found that incorrect information is being reported.

My account at XYZ Company, account #111111, was paid in full as agreed and is not a charge-off. Please remove this.

I have never paid Kelly Company 60 days late, account #12344. Please correct this.

Tax lien docket #555555 was paid in full. I do not owe that.

My name is John Doe and I reside at 2233 Park Ave., Anytown, CA 22222. My Social Security number is 111-22-3333. My previous address was 6143 Summer Lane, Anytown, CA 22222. My birthdate is 11-17-50.

Sincerely,

John Doe

PERSONALIZE YOUR LETTER!!!

The credit reporting agencies will complete their investigation with the creditors within 30 days after receiving the letter explaining your dispute. If the creditors fail to respond to the credit bureau within those 30 days, the disputed item or items must be removed from the credit file by federal law. If a disputed item is unverifiable or incorrect, it must be corrected or removed from the credit report.

You should receive a copy of your updated credit report within 45 to 60 days after mailing your letter, and it should indicate any changes.

## Sample Dispute Letter—Form #2B

(Notice Date 30 days later)                                    July 19, 1996

Dear Credit Bureau,

After receiving my credit report and checking my records, I have found infor-mation that is not correct. My name is John Doe and I reside at 2233 Park Ave., Anytown, CA 22222. My Social Security number is 111-22-3333. My previous address was 6143 Summer Lane, Anytown, CA 22222. My birthdate is 11-17-50.

I do not have an account with Brewer's Collection, account #12456. My account at Nelson's Department Store, #4441, was paid in full as agreed and should have a positive rating.

Bankruptcy docket #45667 for $100,000, 10-12-88, is wrong and should not be on my report. It is not mine.

Sincerely,

John Doe

### PERSONALIZE YOUR LETTER!!!

**Step 3:** When you receive a copy of your updated credit report, note what changes were made. Occasionally, not all the incorrect items are removed the first time, but you should see some changes. Do not be dis-couraged. Repeat Step 2. Dispute only the remaining incorrect items on the credit report and mail the letter 120 days after the last updated report you receive. You can repeat this procedure as often as you want, but it is important to space the letters properly.

If you don't wish to continue the letter writing on any items remain-ing on the report, you can attach a 100-word statement to each incorrect entry that remains, explaining your side of the story. (See Sample 100-Word Statement to Credit Bureau.)

## Things to Remember

1. Request credit reports from the appropriate agencies.
2. Enclose the correct fee for the reports if there is no denial of credit.
3. Husband and wife must request credit reports separately.
4. Analyze all negative, inaccurate, incomplete information.
5. If the credit reporting agency has dispute forms, use its form; if not, write a letter guided by Sample Dispute Form #2A.
6. Personalize your letter; write it by hand and use your own words.
7. Make sure all letters include the date.
8. Review all updated reports.
9. Repeat the request process if necessary.
10. Be patient and persistent.

## Payment History

The following descriptions are used to indicate the most common kinds of payment history shown on a credit report:

CURRENT ACCOUNT—Open or closed account in good standing

INQUIRY—Consumer's credit information requested by a merchant or other business

CLOSED ACCOUNT—Credit account closed

PAID ACCOUNT—Closed account with zero balance

CREDIT ACCOUNT REINSTATED—Previously closed account now available to consumer

JUDGMENT—Court judgment entered against consumer but not paid

CHARGE-OFF—Credit amount cannot be collected

REPOSSESSION—Charged items returned to merchant

CUR WAS 30, 60, 90 DAYS—Account current; was 30, 60, 90 days late

COLLECTION ACCOUNT—Credit account assigned to collection agency for collection

BANKRUPTCY—Bankruptcy file

TAX LIEN—Amount owed the Internal Revenue Service or state, city, or county revenue departments

The credit reporting agencies must respond to any disputed entry sent to them within a reasonable time unless they feel it is frivolous or irrelevant. The credit bureaus will complete their investigation with the creditors within 30 days from receipt of your letter. If the creditors don't respond within that time frame, the disputed entry will be removed from your credit report. *Don't offer a fictitious story.* What you are trying to do is initiate an investigation into inaccurate information being reported on your credit file so that it will be removed or corrected. The sample responses above can be used or you can write one more appropriate for your situation. The more you project your personality, the better the letter.

## Reestablishing Credit after a Bankruptcy

After going through a bankruptcy or any other severe financial hardship, you may feel that ever getting new credit is hopeless. The good news is that with careful planning and strategy you can rebuild your credit.

A bankruptcy remains on your credit report for ten years and other negative information for seven years; however, after a two-year period you can probably rebuild your credit.

When a creditor is reviewing your credit application, it looks for steady employment, a history of your paying habits, your credit report, and checking and savings accounts established since your financial crisis. You are probably wondering how you can get a positive history of your paying habits when you lost everything. By following the suggestions below, you should be able to build up your credit report once again.

A word of caution: Make sure that the financial crisis you are coming out of has ended. You may not be ready to enter the world of credit again. Overspending can be just as hard to overcome as gambling or excessive drinking. Some people are hooked on credit card spending.

### *Debtors Anonymous*

Debtors Anonymous is a support program similar to Alcoholics Anonymous. They have programs nationwide. Even if you are not hooked on spending, it may be worth your time to get information on the program. You can write to the organization to find out where there is a group in your area. Send a self-addressed, stamped envelope to: Debtors Anonymous, General Services Board, P.O. Box 400, Grand Central Station, New York, NY 10163-0400; or call 212-642-8220 for a recorded message on how to obtain more information.

Here are suggestions for reestablishing your credit.

**Secured credit cards.**   Applying for a secured credit card will help you reestablish yourself. It is done by setting up an account with a bank or savings and loan association that offers secured credit cards. (Review the section in Chapter 2 on secured credit cards.)

**Unsecured credit cards.**   Some banks now offer unsecured credit cards (meaning no deposit is necessary) to assist individuals in reestablishing credit. To qualify, you must be employed, provide proof of telephone or utility bills, have a certain income, and have no recent derogatory credit entries within the past six months. For details and an application, contact Professional Credit Counselors, 1100 Irvine Blvd., #541, Tustin, CA 92780; 714-541-2637.

**Merchants.**   Many times local merchants can help you reestablish your credit. Explain your situation to them. They may have special programs available to you. They may require a large deposit and a high interest rate. Find out if they report your payment activity to a credit bureau. If they approve you for a purchase, pay the item back within 90 days if possible. If you are paying a high interest rate, you want to pay off the balance as soon as possible. You are only trying to improve your credit rating.

**Automobile.**   There are dealers that specialize in selling cars to people who have been bankrupt or have bad credit. Check your telephone directory, or look for advertisements of car dealers that specialize in these types of problems. Be prepared to pay a large deposit and a high interest rate. The automobile you buy is the collateral for the loan, so many dealers are interested in helping you. Be sure to make your payments on time to build up your credit report.

**Savings account.**   Open a savings account and use the money you have deposited as collateral to secure a small loan. Pay the loan on time. Make sure the bank reports the activity on your credit report. When you apply for new credit, creditors like to see that you have a savings account. By having a savings account and securing it with a loan and a good payment pattern, you have accomplished two things.

**Mortgage after two years.** Many mortgage companies will grant a mortgage to someone two years after the person filed for bankruptcy. They want to see new credit that is in good standing. Before you look for a new home, have a lender prequalify you to make sure you can get a loan. Be open and honest about your past so the lender can get you the best possible loan for your situation.

Reestablishing your credit will take some time. It is not an overnight process, but it can be done. Be patient and persistent.

---

## Sample Responses

1. I do not recall having this account; it is not mine.
2. I do not believe I was ever 30, 60, or 90 days late on this account.
3. I paid this account in full as agreed; it was not a charge-off.
4. This is not my bankruptcy (insert date and amount).
5. I do not owe this judgment for $ _amount_ .
6. I do not owe this tax lien for $ _amount_
7. This account was the responsibility of my separated or divorced spouse.

## Sample 100-Word Statement to Credit Bureau

October 13, 1996

To Whom It May Concern,

Please add this statement to my credit profile. Make it a part of my credit report.

In May 1994, I was laid off my job due to an injury. I fell behind on my payments. It took me four months to get back to my job, but my debts had become seriously delinquent. I made arrangements with my creditors to repay the debts. I have since paid them all off and am in good standing. My job is secure and I am now trying to rebuild my credit.

My name is John Smith. I reside at 2398 Main St., Anytown, MN 33333. My Social Security number is 333-88-9999. My previous address was 1245 Maple, Anytown, MN 33444. My birthdate is 5-9-44.

Sincerely,

(Sign name)

## Credit Report Questionnaire Worksheet

From the list below, select the appropriate statements regarding your account
to assist you in writing your letters to the credit reporting agencies.

Creditor's name

_____
_____
_____
_____
_____
_____
_____
_____
_____
_____
_____
_____

1. This is not my account.
2. The payment was not late as indicated.
3. The debt was not charged off.
4. The debt was paid in full as agreed.
5. The account was not a collection account.
6. This is not my bankruptcy as indicated.
7. This is not my tax lien as indicated.
8. This is not my judgment as indicated.

## Tracking Dispute Letters Worksheet

Enter the dates on which you sent your "dispute" letters to the credit bureaus. Indicate when you received your updated credit report.

| Date | Bureau Name | Date Updated Report Received |
|---|---|---|
| | | |
| | | |
| | | |
| | | |
| | | |
| | | |
| | | |
| | | |
| | | |
| | | |
| | | |
| | | |
| | | |
| | | |

## Credit Update Worksheet

List the credit bureaus and items you have disputed on your credit report. When you receive your updated credit report, indicate the results.

| Credit Bureau Name | Account Disputed | Status | | |
|---|---|---|---|---|
| | | Removed | Corrected | Remain |
| | | | | |
| | | | | |
| | | | | |
| | | | | |
| | | | | |
| | | | | |
| | | | | |
| | | | | |
| | | | | |
| | | | | |
| | | | | |
| | | | | |
| | | | | |
| | | | | |

# Chapter 11

# The Most Frequently Asked Questions and Their Answers

### 1. Do the credit bureaus rate my credit?

No! The credit bureaus are not allowed to rate your creditworthiness. They only report the information they receive from their subscribers. They cannot approve or disapprove any credit requests.

### 2. What is not reported on my credit report?

A credit report does not include information regarding race, religion, gender, salary, personal assets, checking or savings accounts, medical history, personal background, or lifestyle.

### 3. How long does a negative entry stay on my report?

A negative entry can remain on your credit report for up to seven years. Bankruptcies remain up to ten years. Such entries remain from the date of the reported delinquency.

### 4. Why don't all my accounts show up on my credit report?

The subscribers on these accounts may not be members of the particular credit bureau that sent you a report.

### 5. When I look in the phone book, I see several credit reporting bureaus. How do I know which one to go to?

There are three major credit reporting agencies in the United States—Experian, Trans Union, and Equifax. The credit bureaus listed in the phone book obtain their information from one of the three major bureaus and enter it on the forms they sell to local credit grantors. If you need a credit report, find out from these smaller agencies where they get their information.

### 6. How did I become part of a credit bureau's file?

When you first began to apply for credit, you signed at the bottom of your contract an authorization for the credit grantor to report credit information to the credit reporting agencies. In addition, you authorized the grantor to run a credit report on you. Once you provided your name, address, Social Security number, and birthdate, a file was set up.

### 7. Is my wife's file a part of mine?

No! Each person has his or her own separate credit report based on that person's Social Security number, name, and address. You must request a separate report for your wife and for yourself.

### 8. Does the government have access to my file?

Yes! Any debt owed the government—federal, state, or local—allows it access to your credit profile.

### 9. What information is needed for me to obtain my credit report?

Your full name, current address, addresses for the past five years, Social Security number, and birth date. Include two forms of identification, such as your drivers license, a utility bill, or a credit card statement with your name and address.

### 10. Are debts that have been paid kept in my credit report?

Yes, your credit grantors report good credit on your credit report. Creditors use that information when evaluating your credit report. Accounts that have been paid off remain on the credit report for seven years from the last payment or last activity on the account.

### 11. Why was I turned down on my credit application?

Credit bureaus don't make credit-granting decisions. They only supply your payment history, which is reported to them by a credit grantor you have had an account with.

The credit grantor you have applied to for credit is the party that makes the decision whether to grant you credit. Its decision is based on such factors as your payment history, income, and employment. If you do not qualify on the basis of the grantor's criteria, the grantor will reject your loan application.

### 12. What do inquiries from other companies mean on my credit report?

An inquiry noted on your credit report means that you authorized the company named in the report to run a credit report on you for checking your credit history. The entry on the credit report lists the name of the company and the date of the inquiry.

Excessive inquiries made within a six-month period may hinder your chances of obtaining new credit. An inquiry is usually deleted two years after the date it is reported.

# Epilogue

The information contained in this book can help you gain knowledge in all areas of credit. By completing the worksheets, you will be able to decide what areas you need to improve as well as having pertinent information at your fingertips when dealing with credit issues.

You want to always have a plan. Don't take for granted that things will always be the way they are today. Things do change. The best way to avoid credit problems is to not get in over your head and think you can escape paying your debts. If you cannot afford it today, wait until you can. Going into debt can happen so quickly that you do not realize when it is sneaking up on you. Being debt free is the best thing for you to be, although it is a difficult thing to accomplish. You can do it by following your plan of action.

Always be concerned about your credit report. Once you have cleared it of inaccuracies, make it a habit to order copies of your report at least once every six months to a year. Always be aware of what your rating is. You never know when you may need credit.

If your financial situation is totally out of control, seek the advice of an attorney who can advise you on your best options.

Establishing credit, restoring credit reports, and dealing with credit problems are not overnight processes. It takes time to accomplish results. Do not be impatient. Just do your part.

# Appendix A
## Federal Government Publications

The Federal Trade Commission offers many publications about consumer credit free of charge. The following are publications and laws pertaining to credit that you can request from the commission:

- Building a Better Credit Record
- Cosigning a Loan
- Credit and Charge Card Fraud
- Credit and Older Americans
- Credit-Billing Errors
- Credit Practices Rule
- Equal Credit Opportunity Act
- Fair Credit Billing Act
- Fair Debt Collection Practices Act
- Home Equity Credit Lines
- Mortgage Money Guide: Creative Financing for Home Buyers
- Refinancing Your Home
- Scoring for Credit
- Second Mortgage Financing
- Solving Credit Problems
- Women and Credit Histories
- Fair Credit Reporting Act

These publications can be obtained by writing to the Federal Trade Commission, Public Reference Dept., 6th and Pennsylvania Ave., NW, Washington, DC 20580.

# Appendix B

## Regional Offices of the Federal Trade Commission

Federal Trade Commission
26 Federal Plaza
New York, NY 10278

Federal Trade Commission
118 St. Clair Ave.
Cleveland, OH 44114

Federal Trade Commission
1718 Peachtree St. NW
Atlanta, GA 30367

Federal Trade Commission
450 Golden Gate Ave.
San Francisco, CA 94102

Federal Trade Commission
55 East Monroe St.
Chicago, IL 60603

Federal Trade Commission
8303 Elmbrook Dr.
Dallas, TX 75247

Federal Trade Commission
150 Causeway St.
Boston, MA 02114

Federal Trade Commission
1405 Curtis St.
Denver, CO 80202

Federal Trade Commission
11000 Wilshire Blvd.
Los Angeles, CA 90024

Federal Trade Commission
915 Second Ave.
Seattle, WA 98174

*Central Office:*
Federal Trade Commission
6th & Pennsylvania Ave., NW
Washington, DC 20580

# Glossary

**annual percentage rate (APR)**  The percentage rate calculated on a yearly basis

**applicant**  Any person who applies to a creditor for credit

**asset**  Property that can be used to repay a debt such as cash, real estate, or personal items

**balance**  The amount owed on an account

**bankruptcy**  The act of having your estate administered under the bankruptcy laws for the benefit of your creditors

**charge card**  A card used to buy goods and services from the issuing merchant on credit with payment usually due in 30 days

**collateral**  Property offered to secure a loan or credit that is subject to seizure in the case of default

**cosigner**  An individual other than an applicant who signs for a loan and assumes equal liability for the debt

**credit**  The promise to pay a sum of money due a person or business in the future to buy or borrow in the present

**credit card**  A card that may be used repeatedly to borrow money or purchase goods and services on credit

**credit contract**  A written agreement between a creditor and debtor

**credit history**  A record of how a person has repaid debts

**credit rating**  An evaluation by a creditor or credit reporting agency that reflects a debtor's credit history and is based on the debtor's payment pattern

**credit reporting agency**  An agency that keeps credit records on individuals

**creditor**  An individual or business that provides credit by lending money or selling goods and services on credit for a promise of repayment

**default**  Failure to meet a financial obligation

**deferred payment**  A payment that can be paid at a later time

**deficiency**  The difference between the amount of money you owe a creditor that has foreclosed on your house or your personal property and the amount of money realized from the sale of the house or property; the amount of the deficiency is owed to the creditor

**exempt property**  A debtor's property that can be excluded from the obligation to pay in a bankruptcy

**finance charge**  The dollar amount assessed for granting credit

**foreclosure**  The right of a creditor that has a lien on your property to force a sale of that property to recover what is owed if you have stopped making payments

**gross income**  The amount of money you earn before taxes and expenses are deducted

**installment contract**  A written agreement to pay for goods or service purchases; it sets forth the terms, such as the payments of principal and interest, and the date of payments

**joint account**  An account that two or more people can use with each assuming the liability to repay the debt

**judgment**  An obligation, such as a debt, created by a court decree that indicates the amount due the suing party

**late payment**  A payment made after the due date

**lien**  The legal right to hold property or to have it sold or applied for the payment of a claim owed a creditor; a lien is usually placed on real estate

**liquidate**  To convert an asset to cash

**net income**  The amount of money left from your paycheck or other sources after taxes and expenses are deducted

**nonpurchase money agreement**  A contract by which you borrow money and pledge certain property for the loan

**purchase money agreement** A contract by which you pledge the property or item you are buying

**refinance** To pay old debts with a new loan

**reinstate a contract** If you fall behind in making your payments, and the property or item is foreclosed or repossessed, you have a period of time to get the property or item back; the property or item would then be reinstated after all the back payments and fees were brought current

**repossession** The act of a creditor reclaiming or taking back property from a consumer who does not fulfill the terms of the contract

**retail credit** Credit offered to customers by merchants for the purpose of allowing them to buy now and pay later

**secured credit card** A major credit card you obtain by opening a savings account with a bank that secures the credit card it issues with your deposit

**secured debt** A specific item used as collateral to guarantee payment

**security agreement** The contract you sign to get a secured loan that indicates the property or other collateral to be taken should you default

**service charge** A fee charged for a particular service that is often in addition to an interest charge

**unsecured debt** A debt that has no collateral to guarantee repayment

# Index

# About the Author

Deborah McNaughton is the founder of Professional Credit Counselors. She is a nationally known credit expert who has been interviewed on hundreds of radio and TV talk shows. Ms. McNaughton's business offers assistance in credit consulting, mortgages, automobile purchases, and financial planning. She is the author of several books on credit, including *Everything You Need to Know about Credit, Have a Good Report,* which she coauthored with John Avanzini, and *The Credit Repair System,* a business opportunity manual that has helped hundreds of credit counseling businesses throughout the United States get started. Ms. McNaughton conducts "Credit and Financial Strategies" seminars nationally and offers a distributorship program of her seminars. In 1990, she founded Inner-Strength International, introducing her motivational workshop and manual "Yes You Can" to help individuals discover their full potential in life by focusing on finances, hope, and encouragement.

To receive more information about the seminars, products, and services, write:

Deborah McNaughton
1100 Irvine Blvd., #541
Tustin, CA 92780
714-541-2637